Resurre<

A. M. Allchin is Honorary Professor in the University of Wales in Bangor and has written extensively in the fields of theology and contemporary spirituality. His publications include *Joy of All Creation – an Anglican Meditation on the place of Mary, Praise Above All*, and *God's Presence Makes the World*.

Resurrection's Children

Exploring the way towards God

A. M. Allchin

Foreword by the Archbishop of Wales

CANTERBURY
PRESS
Norwich

© A. M. Allchin 1998

First published in 1998 by The Canterbury Press
Norwich (a publishing imprint of Hymns Ancient &
Modern Limited a registered charity)
St Mary's Works, St Mary's Plain
Norwich, Norfolk, NR3 3BH

All rights reserved. No part of this publication which
is copyright may be reproduced, stored in a retrieval
system, or transmitted, in any form or by any means,
electronic, mechanical, photocopying, recording, or
otherwise, without the prior permission of the publisher.

A. M. Allchin has asserted his right under the
Copyright, Designs and Patents Act, 1988, to be
identified as Author of this work.

British Library Cataloguing in Publication Data

A catalogue record for this book is available
from the British Library

ISBN 1-85311-236-4

Typeset by Rowland Phototypesetting,
Bury St Edmunds, Suffolk
Printed in Great Britain by
Biddles Ltd, Guildford and King's Lynn

Cyflwynir yr llyfr hwn
I'r Parchedig Robert Williams
Rheithor Llangwnnadl 1955–1990
Canon Eglwys Gadeiriol Bangor 1984–1990

* * *

Rhoist i ni ar weundir amser
Llewyrch yr anfeidrol awr,
Ailgynheaist yn ein hyspryd
Hen gyfathrach nef a llawr.

Contents

Foreword by the Archbishop of Wales ix
Introduction xi

1. Cheerfully Towards Jerusalem: *Williams Pantycelyn and the Hymns of Wales* 1
2. Companions on the Way: *Mary Jones, Ann Griffiths and Ruth Evans* 17
3. The Harvest of Maturity: *Waldo Williams* 35
4. On the Roads of Wales: *D. Gwenallt Jones* 54
5. Stages of Life's Journey: *Guto'r Glyn* 73
6. The Isle of Expectation: *Meilyr Brydydd* 90
Conclusion: *The End which is a Beginning* 108

Appendix: *Things to Discuss and Places to Visit* 114
Notes 119

Foreword

by Alwyn Rice Jones, Archbishop of Wales.

For many years I have been aware of the Reverend Canon A. M. Allchin's deep and unflinching interest in Welsh spirituality. For him as an Englishman this has meant learning Welsh in order to grapple with the intricacies of Welsh literature – poetry and prose.

Spirituality for him can be defined as an effort to live in the life of our understanding of God through Jesus Christ in the power of the Holy Spirit.

This book therefore is a great "summing up" of his developing interest over the years and which he readily imparts with a great many of us.

In these pages his interest in Welsh spirituality is identified with prominent Welsh theologians, evangelists, hymnologists and people of letters right down the centuries.

It is good that he has been willing to share with us his appreciation of Welsh culture through his insight into the spirituality of Wales.

May you join me in enjoying this valuable book in your preparation for Easter.

Alwyn Rice Jones, Archbishop of Wales
Lent 1999

Introduction

When I was invited to write the Archbishop of Wales' Lent Book for 1999, my mind at once went to the basic shape and movement of Lent. Lent begins on Ash Wednesday with the reminder of our mortality. The words in the old Liturgy which were said as the ashes were put on our foreheads – 'Remember, O Man, that dust thou art and unto dust shalt thou return' – are not easily forgotten.

But what begins in dust and ashes comes in time to the conflict between life and death which we celebrate in Holy Week; and that reaches its climax in the celebration of Easter night, when time and again we affirm with the Eastern Church that 'Christ is risen from the dead, trampling down death by death and to those in the tombs giving life.' The journey of Lent is a journey from time to eternity, from death to life, from slavery to freedom.

In this book I have tried to illustrate this basic affirmation with material taken from the long history of Christian Wales. I have tried to see how the pattern of Lent applies to our life as a whole, in a great variety of ways. Perhaps inevitably I have begun with the one Welsh hymn which is widely known throughout the English-speaking world, Williams Pantycelyn's, 'Guide me O Thou Great Jehovah'.

In this hymn Pantycelyn uses the Old Testament account of the Exodus – the journey of the people of Israel from slavery in Egypt up through the desert into the freedom of the promised land – as a model and pattern for the journey

Resurrection's Children

of the Christian through this world of space and time into the great world which lasts forever. It is a journey which God's people make together, yet it is in the end a journey which each one must make on his or her own. In a masterly way Pantycelyn shows us how the saving acts of God in history become, through Christ in the worship of the Church, saving acts of God today.

In Chapter 2 we stay with the beginnings of Welsh Methodism and think of the way in which actual journeys, regularly made to great gatherings for preaching and worship, played a central role in the growth of the movement. We think of the importance of Llangeitho in the early years in the South, and of Bala later in the North. We look at the stories of three young women who, just 200 years ago, were deeply influenced by these journeys to Bala. One of them, Ann Griffiths, became a great hymn-writer, and we consider how her hymn about Christ the Way sees our life as moving from the shadows and perplexities of time into the fulfilment and joy of God's eternity.

In Chapters 3 and 4 we pass from the eighteenth century into the twentieth, and we see the way in which two of the outstanding Christian poets of the middle years of this century treat our theme. Waldo Williams is a natural contemplative, perhaps we could say a natural mystic. For him, the journey of life is as much an inward as an outward thing, a way of spiritual growth and discovery. We look at two of his poems which show us the Christian character, at the end of the journey through life, as something completed and fulfilled. We see this fulfilment in the conjunction of grief and joy, of prayer and concern, in the life of Waldo's mother Angharad. We see it again in the conjunction of inner insight with social and pastoral activity in the life of his friend Llwyd Williams.

Gwenallt, Waldo's contemporary, was a very different

Introduction

character, a man more directly involved in the conflicts and movements of his day. His journey from childhood faith, through rebellion and rejection of belief, into the evangelical Catholicism, the deeply Christian socialism of his maturity, is made with full awareness of the changing circumstances of his times, both national and international.

These were times which saw the devastation of World War I, the economic disaster of the inter-War years, the rise of fascism in Western Europe, and the dominant position of communism in the world after World War II. All this is reflected in Gwenallt's personal journey; it is also reflected in his poem on St David, whom he sees still journeying through Wales, with the gospel and the altar in his caravan: for 'there is no barrier between two worlds in the Church'.

In Chapters 5 and 6 we go back in time to the Middle Ages, to a time when the actual practice of pilgrimage was a regular part of Christian life. We look first at a writer of the fifteenth century, Guto'r Glyn, a man who was as much involved in the movements of his own time as Gwenallt would be in his 500 years later. Guto was a poet who shows us in his work the different stages of a long life, from youth, through middle age, into a lengthy and active old age. He shows us a deeply compassionate response to the advent of tragic injury into a life of action. It is this which makes him issue a call to go on pilgrimage to one of the ancient holy places in Wales, Pennant Melangell, a place which has come to life again in the last decade.

Other aspects of the meaning of pilgrimage are explored in Chapter 6, which takes us further back into the past to Bardsey Island or Ynys Enlli, one of the most famous pilgrimage places of Wales. Throughout the Christian centuries Enlli has been known as the island of the saints, the island of death and resurrection. The pilgrimage which Meilyr Brydydd, court poet to the Prince of Gwynedd,

Resurrection's Children

prays to make to that place is both personal and public. It takes us to this island, a place which is at once near yet far, accessible yet inaccessible, a place which people today are once again finding to be a place of 'the little resurrection'.

Thus we look at different aspects of our theme – life as a journey with Christ, lived towards death, and through death into life. In a brief Conclusion which takes us beyond Lent into the period of Easter, we consider the meaning of Christ's resurrection in the light of the services for Easter night in Eastern and Western Christendom. These services present us with the faith of the first millennium of the Christian era, the period in which the specific tradition of the Celtic countries was formed. They show us Easter as new life from the tomb, not only for the individual but for the whole creation.

At the end of each chapter some topics for discussion are suggested, which may be useful when the book is used for study by a group. Apart from the specific topics suggested in these questions, there are a number of other themes which recur throughout the book, raising issues which can touch our own lives in practical ways.

The first of these themes relates to the book's title, *Resurrection's Children*. There is a reference here to the words of Jesus in St Luke's Gospel about the life of the world to come, in which we are to share fully in God's eternal life as sons and daughters of the resurrection (Luke 20:36). But there is also a reference to the way in which some early Christian writers speak of our present life here and now as 'the little resurrection'. This suggests very clearly, as St John's Gospel also implies, that eternal life is not something only in the future. It is something which, at least in part, we know already in this life now, as Ann Griffiths saw clearly. Already we may feel the pressure of eternity

Introduction

upon us; already eternity seems to make itself known in time. When we deeply know or love another person, there seems to be a quality of life between us to which time is irrelevant.

Another theme which is to be found in different contexts in this book is to do with the importance of friendship in Christian life. This may be the kind of friendship which we see in Chapter 2 – a friendship which binds together a group of young people who share their faith and prayer together and long to do some great work for the Lord. It may be the kind of life-long friendship which we find described in Chapters 5 and 6 – friendship which may take many forms and may become very deep. Our way through life may be known as a journey, but it is not for the most part a solitary journey. We need companions on the way, and we are happy indeed when God gives them to us.

The book as a whole takes up this idea of life as a journey, and gives examples of the ways in which people have experienced it in former times. What about our experience of life now at the end of the twentieth century? Is the thought of life as a journey one which is helpful to us? Have there been definite moments in my life, which I can put my finger on, when my life has taken a new direction, or when I have felt one period coming to an end and a new one beginning? Or has my experience of things been more gradual, a process in which change comes slowly and imperceptibly, so that it is only as I look back afterwards that I can see how much things have altered for me, and how much I myself may have altered?

Undoubtedly different people experience their life in very different ways. But perhaps all of us need to recognize that in the course of a lifetime – and many people now live much longer than people used to live – there will be different stages which have their own particular gifts and

Resurrection's Children

callings. Perhaps I can illustrate what I mean by speaking of one particular time of life which has caught my attention more and more as I have got older. This is the period which comes at the end of life, when most of us find that we have far less physical energy than we had before, and we often experience outward limitations and handicap. What is the meaning of these last years, and do they have inner possibilities which are often not recognized?

As I mentioned before, this question is one which presses on our society partly because many people live longer than was usual in earlier times. It is also partly because our society is so focused on outer activities, on our abilities in work or business, on our capacity for making money and having influence on others, that we desperately undervalue the inner possibilities of life which are present, but often hidden, in quite ordinary people and which can sometimes flourish in these last years.

I was first struck by this forty years ago when I was a curate in a large London parish with many old people, often housebound, to whom the clergy would regularly take Holy Communion. I still remember one old lady in her eighties, confined to bed, who had on the wall facing her a whole series of passport-size photographs of her children and grandchildren, her nephews and nieces and their offspring, as well as the friends and neighbours of a lifetime. She was still living in them, living through her love and concern for them, and I couldn't help wondering how much it may have meant to some of them at moments of difficulty or distress to know that Granny or Auntie or old Mrs K. was praying for them. It was an impressive example of how a life in which prayer for other people has been regular and significant can grow and blossom at the very end.

Since then, for much of my life as a priest, I have had

Introduction

the privilege of close contact with communities of contemplative nuns. There again I have seen the same thing – this inner potential of the last decades of life. These are people pushing into their eighties or nineties who take as their motto T. S. Eliot's words, 'Old men ought to be explorers,' and add, 'Yes, and old women too.'

A life in which prayer and prayerful reading have been central can go on to further exploration in these last decades. New writers are discovered, old classics of Christian prayer and thought are rediscovered and re-read, with the new insights which long experience of life gives, sharpened by a sense of drawing nearer to the edge of eternity. There can be great inner freedom and daring in extreme old age. These new explorations are by no means only in the world of books and meditation. I think of one Sister whose whole personal and spiritual life was transformed in her late seventies by a totally unexpected experience of Pentecost within. Rebirth is not a thing reserved for youth! We seriously underestimate the gifts which can be given in old age.

Of course, this is not always the case. The outward restrictions and limitations brought about by growing physical incapacity are sometimes accompanied by inner afflictions such as memory loss or Alzheimer's disease – conditions which seem to change the whole personality. Sometimes one simply witnesses a gradual loss of consciousness of other people and surroundings. But even here, an obstinate faith that God is still present at the heart of such an outwardly stunted life can help one to give value to those last years and to believe that they may not be so inwardly barren as they appear to be from outside.

I have spoken of this particular stage in life's journey here in the introduction, not at all because the book is

Resurrection's Children

concerned exclusively with the problems and possibilities of old age. What is written here will, I hope, be of relevance to people at many different stages in life's journey. But it is true that throughout the book the importance of our inner growth and development is stressed. That is something where age in some ways seems almost irrelevant. Someone may come to great spiritual maturity when still in their twenties, as in the case of Ann Griffiths. Some may remain full of life and imagination even in extreme old age, as we can see in the case of Guto'r Glyn. The possibilities of human life when lived in fellowship with God are much greater than we are often tempted to think.

At the end of the book there are also suggestions for things that might be done, in particular for journeys which might be made to some of the places mentioned in these pages. Just as there is no substitute for actually meeting people face to face, so there is no substitute for actually going to visit a place and, if possible, going at least part of the way on foot. The practice of pilgrimage is something which has reinstated itself in Britain and Northern Europe in the twentieth century in spontaneous and unplanned ways. People have found themselves drawn to kneel at places where prayer has been valid, and where they have found, as Eliot wrote, that

> ... what the dead had no speech for, when living,
> They can tell you being dead; the communication
> Of the dead, is tongued with fire beyond the language
>   of the living.

*

During the last stages of the preparation of this book I have had the privilege of taking part in the rites of Holy Week and Easter in the Cathedral Church of Salisbury.

Introduction

What I had written in these pages acquired new relevance for me through the experience of that week, with the newly restored rites of Holy Week celebrated with such power and beauty, with such simplicity and joy.

A. M. Allchin

Easter 1998

Chapter 1

Cheerfully Towards Jerusalem
Williams Pantycelyn

I
Introduction

Everybody knows that the Welsh sing hymns at rugby matches. This is one of the very few things that most people do know about them. More even than in England, popular hymns have survived in Wales and have defied the recent processes of secularization. Why this should be it is difficult to say; how significant it is, is something about which people differ. No-one can deny, however, that there are still some hymns which can stir popular emotion in surprising ways.

The tune which the Welsh most often sing on such occasions is called *Cwm Rhondda*, 'Rhondda Valley'. It is a tune which is familiar to English people because in England it is regularly sung to well-known words by the best-known of Welsh hymn-writers, Williams Pantycelyn. It is indeed the only Welsh-language hymn which has been successfully translated and has found its way into English hymn books:

> Guide me, O thou great Jehovah,
> Pilgrim through this barren land:
> I am weak but though art mighty,
> Hold me with thy powerful hand.

Resurrection's Children

Bread of heaven,
Feed me till I want no more.

Open now the crystal fountain,
Whence the healing stream doth flow;
Let the fire and cloudy pillar
Lead me all my journey through.
Strong deliverer,
Be thou still my strength and shield.

When I tread the verge of Jordan
Bid my anxious fears subside;
Death of death and hell's destruction,
Land me safe on Canaan's side.
Songs of praises
I will ever give to thee.[1]

I had sung this hymn for decades before, one day, I suddenly noticed how closely it follows the story to be found in the Book of Exodus, the story of the journey made by the people of Israel from captivity in Egypt to the promised land of Canaan on the other side of the river Jordan. This journey from slavery to freedom is one which, in the biblical narrative, takes forty years – a whole lifetime. And this is not just a matter of ancient history. The hymn is a typical and beautiful example of the way in which the eighteenth-century hymn-writers, both in Welsh and in English, could handle the Bible in a very traditional way, a way which has been followed through all the changes in Christian history. They saw the Bible as a book of stories which were not only of the past but also of the present. It was a book which had not just one meaning but many. Its stories reached out and gathered its readers in, so that they became involved in the sequence of events described. In such a way of seeing things, past, present and future can

Cheerfully Towards Jerusalem

come together, and reading and experience can interact.

Doubtless, the first thing we see in this hymn is the Old Testament history itself, as told in the Book of Exodus. In the Welsh original (which is longer than the English version) the details of the journey of the people through the wilderness are set out more clearly than they are in the English wording, where at times they have been somewhat telescoped together.[2] In the third verse in the Welsh version, for instance, the column of fire which leads the people at night-time and the pillar of cloud which leads them through the day are more sharply distinguished. They are mentioned first as the means of God's providential guidance of his people; only then comes the reference to the manna, the heaven-sent food which sustains the people on their journey and which, in the English version, finds its way into the preceding verse. Again, in the Welsh version, the springs of sweet water, which heal and restore, which mysteriously follow the people through the wilderness ('they drank of that spiritual rock that followed them: and that rock was Christ', 1 Corinthians 10:4 (AV)), have a whole verse to themselves, and their meaning is more fully explored.

But the basic themes of the hymn remain the same both in Welsh and in English. It is not only a hymn about the past; it is a hymn about today. It is not only about the people of Israel but about God's people now. Moreover, it is not only about a whole people but about each one of us in our own situation.

It begins with the weakness and powerlessness of the pilgrim and his need to trust himself wholly to the power of God. At its climax it affirms this very same thought. When the people arrive at the river Jordan they can only cross in the power of God. Just as their journey began with the miracle of the crossing of the Red Sea, so here a no less vital crossing must be made. Only God can take them

3

Resurrection's Children

through this river, which is, as one immediately discovers, nothing less than the river of death.

Already, in our first attempt to unravel the language of the hymn, we find that the Old Testament story of the journey is becoming our story. The congregation which sings the hymn and the individual who joins in the singing are being encouraged to identify themselves with the story and to make it their own. It speaks not only in corporate terms, of the destiny of the whole people, but also in an intimately personal way which touches each one.

All this is possible because in a Christian perspective the story is, in the end, focused in Christ himself. The Old Testament story is interpreted through the New Testament, and the whole of the New Testament is understood as gathered together in the person of Jesus. The healing stream which flows from the rock in the wilderness becomes the water which flows from the side of Christ on the cross; and this, we find, is nothing other than the water of baptism in which the believer receives new birth. The pillar of fire and the pillar of cloud which lead us on our way point us to the overshadowing of the Spirit's presence, for the Church and for each believer. It is he who is our guardian and guide. The pattern here is implicitly, if not explicitly, trinitarian. The Spirit leads us on, as Pantycelyn says in another hymn:

> Come Holy Spirit, fire by night,
> Pillar of cloud by day;
> Lead me, I dare not take a step,
> Unless you show the way.[3]

Again, the heavenly bread with which we are fed is the bread of the Eucharist – the food for pilgrims, nourishment for those who are travelling through this world which passes away, towards the great world which lasts for ever.

In both the Welsh and the English versions of the hymn,

Cheerfully Towards Jerusalem

the climax comes in the lines in which each one is called to face the river Jordan, the way into the promised land. In both versions it is clear that it is only in Christ's strength that we can undertake this crossing. In the English wording, our fears are overcome as we call upon the one who is himself the death of death and the conqueror of hell. This is the triumphant Christ who, by his death, has destroyed death and who, by his rising to life again, has restored to us everlasting life. In the Welsh version, as we reach the river, we find cruel death, in all its strength, awaiting us. But because Jesus has gone through the flood before us, we have no need to fear – indeed, we can shout 'Victory!' as we pass through the floods. In Welsh the word for 'victory' is *buddugoliaeth*. It is one of those weighty, vibrant words which by their very form seem to give substance and solemnity to the Welsh original – words which lend themselves to singing in rousing and triumphant refrains.

The final verse of the hymn in the Welsh original, which does not form part of the English version, is a kind of coda or conclusion to the whole, a personal expression of faith and confidence on the part of the singer. It finally brings us out of the historical matrix in which the hymn was originally formed, into the present day.

> I trust in your power.
> Great is the deed you did once for all;
> You put down death, you put down hell;
> You put down Satan under your feet.
> Hill of Calvary! [*Pen Calfaria!*]
> May this never go from my mind.

On Ynys Enlli (or Bardsey Island), the holy island off the north-west tip of Wales (to which we shall return at the end of this book), there is a tombstone in the graveyard which commemorates one of the principal farmers of the island in the last century, who died in January 1883. The stone gives us his name, the name of his house, the date of his death and his age at the time of death, which was seventy-eight. It then says, very simply, 'His favourite verse was "Pen Calfaria! May this never go from my mind."'

The one thing which Griffith Pritchard, Ty Pellaf, wanted to be recorded about his life, apart from the name of his farm, which means 'Furthest House', was this verse which sums up the whole of the Christian dispensation. As he went about his farm in all weathers, bringing in the animals, digging up the fields, as he steered his little boat across the dangerous waters of the sound, it was this verse that never went from his mind.

Certainly, life on a hill-farm or on an island like Enlli would have been very hard in the nineteenth century. People worked long hours and had few of the material comforts which we take for granted. Yet they sometimes managed to live their lives very much in touch with eternity, and in that they challenge and also encourage us to think what might be possible for us today.

So, our life is a journey; a journey which we make with others but also a journey which we make alone. It is a journey which is rooted in events which happened two or three thousand years ago. But the meaning of the journey is renewed century by century, age by age, not only among Christian people but also among Jewish people whenever they celebrate the Passover. It is a journey in which we are involved today and which certainly is not finished, for it looks forward to the moment when, above all others, we shall have to acknowledge our own powerlessness and entrust ourselves into the hands of the one who has put down death and hell under his feet, the one who leads us through this world of suffering and dismay into the Kingdom where God's glory shines out in all its incontestable majesty.

II
God's beauty draws us

Pantycelyn loves to show us the end of the journey as something which, in a paradoxical way, is already ours now. Yet, no less paradoxically, when we arrive at that end, we shall find that it is itself a new beginning. This end for which we are made, to which we are travelling, is nothing less than to come to God himself – God in his inaccessible glory, God who dwells in light beyond all our perceiving. We come to be made one with him in his infinite goodness, in his infinite truth, but above all – for Pantycelyn – in his infinite beauty. It is the beauty of God which, above all else, draws and empowers us to go forward on the way through life. This is a way which is often difficult, perplexing and apparently without issue, but in Christ we find that it leads to the feast of the Kingdom, the rejoicing of eternity.

So, in a letter of August 1744, written to one of the early Methodist converts, Pantycelyn writes:

> Very dear sister,
> I am glad to hear that you are well – I hope ... that you have the Holy Spirit to lead, guide and govern you; and that your eye is fixed on eternal happiness. It is that that will make you long more and more to be there, and to walk with God continually while here, free from the world and all its pleasure, in an holy fear and an evangelick love ... It is the view of this that increases eternal life in our souls, and makes us become as pilgrims on the earth and go on cheerfully towards the heavenly Jerusalem. My dear sister, there is an ocean of happiness prepared for us and what we experience here is but as a drop or a taste of that which we shall enjoy. A sight of his love is the cause of our love; and our thirst after

him is but the effect of his thirst after us: and our diligence in seeking of him is the effect of his diligence in seeking of us. A sight of this will break our heart and make us look upon ourselves as nothing in his sight . . . Oh that we were always as nothing in his sight! Then indeed he would fashion us as the potter does the clay.[4]

This is a resolutely God-centred view of our passage through life. The initiative is God's at every point. Our part is that of response. As Pantycelyn says, 'It is not our works that is the works of redemption, but the works of Jesus Christ' [sic], The believer is called out of herself or himself into the very life of God, by the ever-growing vision of the love of God taking the initiative in our lives – the beauty of God overwhelming us with its power of attraction. Like all his contemporaries, Pantycelyn makes much use of the imagery and language of the Song of Songs to describe the beauties of God incarnate. He is convinced, as were the theologians of the early Christian centuries and the commentators of the Middle Ages, that this Old Testament text is one of the most precious of all the books in the Bible. It is a text which speaks to us of the depth and power of the love which passes between God and his creation, between God and every human soul.

> Hark, the voice of my beloved,
> Lo he comes to greatest need,
> Leaping on the lofty mountains,
> Skipping over hills with speed,
> To deliver
> Me, unworthy, from all woe.

Or, in another hymn:

> In thy gracious face there's beauty
> Far surpassing everything,

> Found in all the earth's great wonders
> Mortal eye hath ever seen
> Rose of Sharon,
> Thou thyself art heaven's delight.[5]

There is, in Pantycelyn, a remarkable fusion of the divine and the human. There can be no question of the passionate human quality of the love revealed in these hymns. But this love and yearning is always supported and transfigured by the love which comes from God himself. The human response is called out by a vision of the divine compassion – God's willingness to suffer with his creation – which shines out on the hill of Calvary, which shines out in the wounds of the Saviour which bring us healing. Through this narrow point in space, this rubbish-dump outside Jerusalem, through this narrow point in time – 'one afternoon', as Pantycelyn loves to say – all God's love is poured out into our world, and all our human love can be carried up into the vision of God's eternal nature, the beauty of the sacrificial love which lies at the very heart of the Godhead. So, in another hymn Pantycelyn can say:

> If here and now the beauty of your face
> Causes myriads to love you,
> What will your glad beauty do
> There in the expanses of eternity?
> The heaven of heavens
> Will marvel at you ceaselessly forever.
>
> What height will my love reach then,
> What wonder will be mine,
> When I shall see your glory
> Perfect and full on Mount Sion?
> Infinity
> Of all beauties gathered into one.

Resurrection's Children

> What thoughts above understanding
> Shall I find there within myself,
> When I see that the Godhead
> Perfect and pure, and I are one?
> There is a bond
> Which there is no language able to express.[6]

There are many things which need to be said about these verses. First, they speak about a journey, a movement, a transition, which takes us from where we are now, to a height which as yet we cannot imagine. Here already the beauty of Christ's face draws the love of countless multitudes. There, in the fullness of eternity, what will be the power of that beauty? Here already the union of God with his human creature, brought about by the self-emptying love which lies behind the incarnation, prompts thoughts which altogether overwhelm us. There we shall find within ourselves thoughts which take us even further beyond ourselves.

These verses speak of a union and fusion of God with humankind. On the way to that union they pre-suppose a union of human capacities which brings about a wholeness of love and knowledge, an integration of the capacities to love and know which are to be found within the human person. To apprehend the divine glory is not a matter of thought alone or love alone. It demands a fusion of the two. The believer finds himself drawn into an amazed perception of the divine beauty. He is in love with its splendour. At the same time he finds himself full of thoughts which are stirred in his mind by the vision of the faithfulness and truth of God. So love itself gives rise to understanding, and understanding gives rise to love.

This wholeness of love and knowledge reveals itself to be a movement of a radically ec-static kind in which the believer is altogether carried out of himself – or herself.

Cheerfully Towards Jerusalem

We are carried out of ourselves into a union of love and knowledge in which it is no longer we who dominate and control. This is a love and knowledge in which we find that in loving, it is we who are being loved, and in knowing, it is we who are being known. These are forms of love and knowledge which liberate and transform us. For, paradoxically, as we recognize our own nothingness before God, so we are brought into being out of that nothing, and we receive new life from God.

Our society as a whole questions the very possibility of such contemplative, receptive kinds of loving and knowing, in which we are carried out of ourselves and find a love and knowledge beyond our own capabilities. The fact that in the Christian tradition such an experience is very near to the heart of corporate worship, to the Church's life of liturgy, is something which is often overlooked today. The ecstatic dimension of the Church's liturgy is either not recognized at all or thought to be characteristic only of certain kinds of exuberant charismatic worship. But in quieter, and perhaps deeper ways, this ecstatic perception of the divine truth and beauty forms a vital element within the whole tradition of sacramental worship, which is expressed and sustained by gesture and symbolic action, as well as by music and architectural imagery.

Furthermore, this experience is also very near to the innermost place of the practice of silent prayer and meditation, the place where we suddenly discover that we are being taken beyond the point which our own powers could reach, are being taken from active to passive contemplation. But this is also something which is very little acknowledged. Here, too, in the inwardness of prayer there is a way of going beyond concepts and images which takes us beyond ourselves.

It is a tragic fact that for many people in our society words such as 'ecstasy' suggest only going beyond ourselves by the violent and artificial means of drug-taking. Drugs in themselves can never bring about the true integration of the human person, however much they may appear to do so; indeed, they may too easily lead in the reverse direction, to tragic forms of disintegration and destruction.

Pantycelyn not only tells us that we can enter into such forms of love and knowledge in ways which bring about the integration of the human person; he also tells us that it is only in such a movement beyond our own self-centred way of being that we shall find the God-centred life and existence for which humankind was made and in which alone human beings find their fulfilment. In this way, despite his own limitations, Pantycelyn can give us a much more deeply human picture of our life, both in society and as individuals, than that which is projected by our own strangely violent and inhuman world.

As Bobi Jones argues in the chapter on Pantycelyn in his remarkable study of the mystical element in the Welsh religious tradition, the practice of praise which is the very core of his hymnody has a strongly integrating effect in human life. It brings together thought, feeling and the power of action in the world. It is just such an integration which we find in Pantycelyn's own many-sided existence. A poet and hymn-writer, he was at the same time a preacher and teacher, constantly travelling throughout Wales in order to build up the little Methodist societies into a greater maturity of life and experience.[7]

At the end of the verses quoted above Pantycelyn speaks of the bond between human and divine as something which cannot be broken. In the three verses which follow he goes on to speak of it as a bond made in eternity, a mystery as strong and powerful as the mystery of God himself. The bonds of nature, the structures of this world of space and time will, in the end, know dissolution. Here in contrast is a reality whose foundation is deeper than all that belongs to this world which passes away. Here is a design of love rooted for all eternity in the very heart and being of God:

> The bond was made in eternity,
> It is sure, strong, great in power.
> The millions of ages
> Cannot break it or undo it,
> It abides and will abide
> As long as God himself shall last.
>
> The bonds of nature will all be broken,
> Its laws will go for nothing.
> But my union with the heavens
> Is of much greater power;
> It is unchanging,
> Exactly as my God is.
>
> Neither life nor death
> Nor the greatest of the angels,
> Neither cherubim, nor powers,
> Nor all the hosts of heaven above
> Can separate me
> For all eternity from his love.

Here, perhaps, is the deepest point of both the prayer and the faith of this eighteenth-century movement of Calvinistic Methodism in Wales. This is the faith that our union with God is rooted from all eternity in the love which lies at the very heart of God's being. This is the covenant love of the three persons of the Trinity amongst themselves, which overflows into the world in the movement of both creation and redemption. As St Paul affirms in one of the greatest of all his sayings, nothing in the end can separate us from that love of God which is in Christ Jesus (Romans 8:39). Here the geographical extremes of the old Christian world meet. The hymns of Welsh Methodism celebrate in words and poetic images that inmost mystery of the divine love which is presented to us in colour and design in the greatest of Russian icons, the *Holy Trinity* of Andrei Rublev.

III

An eternal and infinite progress

Is this picture of eternity a static and ultimately stultifying one? It is often said that the Christian view of heaven is singularly dull and uninventive. Do we simply sit on clouds and play harps? Such judgements naturally follow from a literal and wooden reading of images which are meant to be alive and many-levelled. For Pantycelyn the mystery of eternity is something already experienced now, but it is necessarily something which opens out towards infinite and eternal horizons.

> Your beauty will be forever new,
> Forever freshly kindling a fire,
> Through all the ages of eternity
> Without ever coming to an end.
> A fervent flame, without ending,
> Through all the ranks of heaven.
> It will continue to burn brightly
> As long as God himself shall endure.[8]

If to participate in God's life is to participate in what is infinite, then there can be no final stopping-place on that journey. In another verse – one of the best known in Welsh – he celebrates the ever-new beginning which this life implies:

> There, there is no end of singing,
> There, there is no end of praise,
> There, there is no end of remembering
> All the tribulations there have been.
> Never shall there be an end
> To the praise of God in my Father's house.[9]

Indeed, it is in the nature of this eternal present that it always involves 'the beginning of singing, the beginning of praise'. Eternity is necessarily and of itself an ever-new beginning, an ever-new movement beyond. So, in the teaching of Gregory of Nyssa, one of the greatest theologians of the early Christian centuries, that eternal life is not to be thought of as something static, but as something that necessarily implies an ever-greater growth – the more we grow, the more we grow. The journey into God is by definition one that has no ending.

Through Pantycelyn's art this faith found new expression in the prayers and praises of the Methodist people of Wales. This was not the esoteric possession of a few; it was, and is, the common inheritance of a multitude.

IV

Hallelujah!

When I first began to learn a little Welsh I was astonished by the number of synonyms there seemed to be for the word 'beauty' – *prydferthwch, harddwch, tegwch* and *tlysni,* for instance. As I began to become familiar with the Old Testament Psalms, following them in Welsh as I sat day by day in my stall at evensong in Canterbury

Cathedral, I was amazed by the weight and substance of the words which refer to the radiance of the divine Kingdom. For 'glory' there is *gogoniant*, for 'splendour' there is *ardderchowgrwydd*, for 'wisdom' there is *doethineb*. You can find the same quality in the keywords of the hymns. Faced with the river of death, the redeemed shout *buddugoliaeth*, and their song goes on through all eternity, *tragwyddoldeb*.[10] Perhaps it is the central role of sacred poetry in the Welsh tradition through the centuries which has gathered together such powerful words – words which seem themselves to be heavy with the weight of glory, presenting us with the very substance of an eternal splendour.

Questions for discussion

1. How far do you think of your own life as a journey? Do you find this a helpful way of reflecting it? Can you see certain turning points, moments when you have passed from one stage to another?

2. Do you think that the Church as a whole sufficiently recognizes the gifts and callings of old people? Could we do more to help them discover the inner meaning and purpose of old age?

3. Pantycelyn speaks much about the beauty of God, and Ann Griffiths insists on the role of words such as 'wonder' and 'astonishment' in our response to God. Do such words as 'beauty' and 'wonder' have a central place in our understanding of Christianity today? If not, should they?

Chapter 2

Companions on the Way
Mary Jones, Ann Griffiths and Ruth Evans

I

Introduction

We have seen how William Williams Pantycelyn took the theme of the journey from slavery in Egypt to freedom in the promised land and used it to speak of the many and varying aspects of our human experience of life, in its changes and vicissitudes. For himself, constantly travelling on horseback through the hills and valleys of Wales, out and about in all weathers, this thought of the solitary traveller became particularly full of meaning. It occurs in many of his greatest hymns.

The Methodist movement in his time – that is, in the period up to 1790 – had been centred in South Wales. Its greatest gathering-point was at Llangeitho, where Daniel Rowland ministered for more than forty years. In the next generation the centre of the movement was in the north, and instead of Llangeitho it was the little town of Bala, at the end of Lake Bala, which was the focus of its life. It was here that Thomas Charles ministered for a similar length of time. He had no less commanding a position in the second phase of the Methodist revival than Daniel Rowland had had in the first.

Resurrection's Children

At Bala, as at Llangeitho, one of the great regular moments of gathering were provided by the monthly Communion Sundays. The Methodist revival was not only a revival of preaching and hymn-singing and enthusiastic extempory prayer; it was also a sacramental revival. Because in the parish churches in Wales at that time the sacrament was celebrated very infrequently – often only three or four times a year – and because the clergy were often men whom the Methodists found it impossible to respect, the converts to the new movement looked forward eagerly to their rare opportunities to share together the sacrament of Communion.

But who was to celebrate the sacrament? Until the moment of actual schism in 1811, the Methodists in Wales remained faithful to the rule that only ordained Anglican priests were qualified to preside at the Lord's table. This meant that celebrations were few, particularly in the North, where there were few Anglican clergy who sympathized with them. It also meant that such moments, when they came, drew together very large congregations and were occasions of great rejoicing.

So, first at Llangeitho and then at Bala, over a period of almost eighty years, the monthly Communion Sundays became moments of great significance, moments which would bring together thousands of worshippers into a long day of singing, preaching, praying, conviviality and sacramental worship. In this chapter I want to look at the place of Bala in the lives of three young women who were all actively involved in the Methodist revival in the North at the end of the eighteenth century and the beginning of the nineteenth. Two of them have achieved a certain fame – Ann Griffiths principally in her own country, and Mary Jones much more widely across the world. The third, Ruth Evans, was, as we shall see, not only Ann's friend and companion, but also the person whose devotion made sure that Ann's work would be remembered by succeeding generations. In the lives of all three, journeys to Bala had an important place, and in the life of Mary Jones there was one particular journey which had overriding significance.

As we study the lives of these three women we cannot help being aware of how much the Anglican Church in Wales lost through the break with Methodism. Of course, there was loss on the Methodist side as well. It is difficult for a self-contained denomination to avoid altogether the dangers of narrowness and rigidity. Both sides had need of one another. This is even more the case today. Now everything speaks to us of the need for reconciliation between the different groupings in the one Christian family and the discovery of new forms of unity.

II

The quest for God's Book

The story of Mary Jones and her Bible is one which has travelled round the world. It has been translated into forty or more languages. It has been received with particular enthusiasm in places where books are very rare and material resources are sparse. It speaks to people who are materially poor but spiritually hungry – hungry and thirsty for knowledge of the true and living God. Upland Wales in the eighteenth century was precisely such a place; although geographically close to England, it was culturally far away. Its people had long and tenacious memories, and they suffered the usual disabilities of those who have to accept colonial status.

It was an area of great material poverty, but it produced

Resurrection's Children

in this period men and women of particular resilience and capability. Gwyn Alf Williams, one of the most brilliant and controversial Welsh historians of our times and a man who had no great love for Methodism, said this part of North Wales, from which Ann, Mary and Ruth came, was

> the most remarkable district of them all. The market at Bala was its focus, and this, the very heartland of Welsh Wales, a land of harsh and sometimes degrading poverty, in which a lively and imaginative people scratched a living with their bare nails, devoted itself with a kind of desperate passion, to the knitting of woollen stockings, which in the seventeen eighties at Bala could produce sales of nearly two hundred thousand pairs at eighteen thousand pounds. From September to March, whole families, to save money on candles, would gather at chosen farmhouses and cottages to knit en masse. The local harpist would cheer them on, storytellers and poets entertained them ... and from the same area, particularly around the district of Bala and Llanuwchllyn, came the popular preachers of non-conformity ... perhaps no area in Wales, except Cardiganshire, was to be such a stronghold. Bala was to be the Mecca of Welsh Methodism.[1]

In this chapter, then, we are going to look at the story of one particular pilgrim to this Mecca. In the form in which it has become popular, it tells of a young girl from a poor family whose longing to possess a Bible is so great that she saves up all she can out of her meagre wages, and eventually walks the twenty-seven miles from her home to Bala in order to see whether Mr Charles can supply one. In at least one version of the story, when she arrives, there are no Bibles to be had, and she has to wait a few days. Thomas Charles arranges a lodging for her, and assures her that some Bibles are on the way. In the end Mary Jones is rewarded for her perseverance and patience. The Bibles do, eventually, come. Sometimes it is said that Charles gave her not one copy but three.

The story, as it has been told, goes on to say that Thomas Charles himself was not only greatly moved by Mary's joy at having a Bible of her own, but was also much impressed by her dedication and quick intelligence. He resolved that the next time he went to London, he would try to stir up his evangelical friends there to found a society which would make the Scriptures available to thousands who had little or no possibility of access to them. His canvassing about this was so successful that it led, in 1804, to the foundation of the British and Foreign Bible Society. For almost two centuries now, this society has worked to make the Bible available in inexpensive editions, not only in Welsh, but in all the languages into which the Scriptures have been translated. It was Mary Jones, with her faith and courage, who, so the story goes, was the ultimate origin of this whole development.

Needless to say, in recent decades there have been those who have questioned the veracity of this story. Perhaps there are details in it which have grown in the telling. Mary Jones' part in the story may have been exaggerated. It is clear that there were others apart from her who were longing to have Bibles. We have, from Charles himself, an eloquent letter of March 1804 which speaks clearly of the longing of many Methodist people to have Bibles of their own:

> The Sunday Schools have occasioned more calls for Bibles within these five years in our poor country than perhaps *ever* was known before among our poor people.... The possession of a Bible produces a feeling among them which the possession of no one thing in

the world besides could produce.... I have seen some of them overcome with joy and burst into tears of thankfulness on their obtaining possession of a Bible as their own property and for their free use. Young females in service have walked thirty miles to me with only the bare hopes of obtaining a Bible each; and returned with more joy and thanksgiving than if they had obtained great spoils. We who have half a dozen Bibles by us, and are in circumstances to obtain as many more, know but little of the value those put upon *one*, who before were hardly permitted to look into a Bible once a week.[2]

When we come to look into the matter in more detail we find that there was a real Mary Jones. She was born and brought up in a hamlet at the head of the Dysynni Valley, at Llanfihangel-y-Pennant. The church in which she was baptized is still there, and she is remembered in it, and so is the site of the cottage where her parents lived. Her father, a landless labourer who earned what he could as a weaver, died in 1789 when Mary was four.

The child grew up as her mother's sole companion. The young widowed woman was already strongly attracted by the teaching of the Methodist movement which was just beginning to be heard in her district. She was a member of the local Methodist *seiat*, the small meeting which brought together believers each week for prayer, study and sharing. Mary herself was admitted at the age of eight, much younger than was usual. This fact may well reflect the little girl's intelligence, and an unusual degree of religious maturity on her part. It must also reflect the situation of the young widowed mother; the child could hardly be left at home during the long winter evenings when the mother was involved in the meetings of the *seiat*.

Mary's famous walk to Bala took place in 1800 when

she was almost sixteen. By that time, she had long since learned to read, and we have a vivid account of her asking and receiving permission to go to a local farmhouse to read the Bible which was there – a permission which depended on her remembering to leave her clogs in the hall. In the precious hour or two allowed to her, she sat and learned Scripture passages by heart.

The first years of the new century saw great activity at Bala. Mary sometimes went there for the summer Association Meetings or for the Communion Sundays. She must have got to know the way over the mountains well; her own two legs would have been her only means of transport. She married in 1813, but of her six children only one survived her, and he had emigrated to the United States. Her life was certainly not without sadness, difficulty and disappointment; her husband died some years before her, and in her later years she lost her sight. She remained, as she had grown up, a poor country woman. When, in the mid-nineteenth century, younger and more prosperous Methodists came to see the old lady whose story was already well known, they were sometimes shocked by her simple, poor, old-fashioned way of doing things.

But we have one picture of her in old age that gives a different flavour to the story. Evidently she kept bees and lived in great harmony with them. Robert Griffith, the minister of the chapel at Bryn-crug where she was a member, described her in these words:

> She had only a small garden, but it was quite full of fruit bushes and innumerable bees, and on a fine summer's day she would be there in the midst of them like a princess, picking them up with her two hands like grains of wheat or barley, without ever one of them making use of its sting to oppose her.

Robert Griffith goes on to tell us that she kept the income from the sale of the honey for her own support, but she divided the money from the wax – a considerable amount – between the Bible Society and the Overseas Mission Society of her church. Her explanation of the fact that the bees never stung her, and that they produced so much honey, and that it was of such good quality, was that they knew that she was devoting a substantial part of their work to the service of their Maker.[3]

Here in the middle of nineteenth-century Wales, at the heart of the Calvinistic Methodist world, we have a picture which might come from the earliest centuries of Celtic Christianity. A woman of prayer and faith, living in harmony with the animate creation, working with God's other creatures in the cultivation of the land which God has given. She is devoting a large part of the produce of that land directly to him. In her poverty she is rich in the gifts of her garden; out of her poverty she finds the means to give to others poorer than herself.

III

The Way that gives us life

Mary Jones was born in the parish of Llanfihangel-y-Pennant, some twenty-seven miles south-west of Bala. Ann Griffiths (Ann Thomas as she was known before her marriage) was born some twenty-two miles south-east of Bala, at Llanfihangel-yng-Gwynfa. Both young women came from parishes dedicated to the chief of archangels, since Llanfihangel simply means 'Church of Michael the Archangel'. From one point of view they had much in common. Both became wholly caught up in the Methodist movement at the time of its greatest fervour in North Wales. Both their lives were shaped and changed by the particular understanding and experience of Christian faith which that movement embodied. Both of them were part of that Welsh-speaking society of the north-west in Meirionydd and Maldwyn which Gwyn Alf Williams described to us so vividly. Ann's family, however, were comparatively well off, and so she knitted stockings not for sale but in order to give them as presents to impoverished preachers. Ann's father had been the church-warden of the parish and her family had a certain standing there. However, their farm was a small one and they belonged entirely to the Welsh-speaking world of the countryside.

There were other differences between Ann and Mary. At a human level, we nearly always see Ann in company with others. She was part of a large, united family. Her mother's death when she was eighteen, with both her elder sisters already married and in homes of their own, left her as mistress of the house at Dolwar. She fulfilled this role until her father's death, looking after him and her two unmarried brothers.

She seems to have had, from the beginning, a leading role amongst the young women of her district. In her pre-conversion days she was a leader in all kinds of exploits and the organizer of parties and evenings of dancing. In her Methodist days she became a leader of a different kind. Above all, she instigated the monthly pilgrimage over the hills to Bala for the Communion Sundays. But while Mary lived on into her late seventies, Ann died before she was thirty. There is a feeling of haste about her life, as if she somehow knew she had not very long to live. She sometimes finished her letters with the words, 'This from your loving sister swiftly travelling through the world of time to the great world which lasts forever.'[4]

Resurrection's Children

The greatest difference between them we have left to the last. It is a simple one. Ann was a genius and a poet. Only two great women poets have been acknowledged in the long history of Welsh literature, and she was one of those two. She was, moreover, a woman of great intellectual and spiritual gifts. If we must call her a mystic – and it seems we can hardly avoid that word – then we must say she was a mystic of a deeply intellectual kind. There can be no doubt about the power of feeling in her hymns, but the power of her intellect may surprise us even more.

For at least 150 years outstanding quality of Ann's hymns has been recognized in the Welsh-speaking world. Recently, it has begun to be acknowledged more widely. For instance, in his first book of poems, *After Silent Centuries*, Bishop Rowan Williams includes two remarkable translations of her work. They are very free and yet also very faithful to the original.

> Wonder is what the angel's eyes hold, wonder:
> The eyes of faith, too, unbelieving in the strangeness,
> Looking on him who makes all being gift,
> Whose overflowing holds, sustains,
> Who sets what is in shape,
> Here in the cradle, swaddled, homeless,
> And here adored by the bright eyes of angels,
> The great Lord recognised.

> Soul, look. This is the place where all kings' monarch
> Rested a corpse, the maker of our rest, and in
> His stillness all things always move
> Within his buried silence.
> Song for the lost, and life; wonder
> For angel's straining eyes, God's flesh.
> They praise together, they adore,
> 'To him', they shout, 'only to him'.[5]

Companions on the Way

More recently Alan Gaunt, the United Reformed Church hymn-writer, has made a translation of all Ann's hymns and verses into singable English. This is a very notable acquisition.[6]

Ann Thomas became Mrs Ann Griffiths in the autumn of 1804. Less than a year later she was dead, two weeks after the birth and death of her only child, a daughter whom she named Elisabeth after one of her two elder sisters. We know very little about that last year of her life. Her husband, Thomas Griffiths, was, like her, an ardent Methodist, a deacon in the Methodist congregation at Meifod. He came from a farming family which was somewhat more affluent than that of Dolwar Fach, and so he brought with him a certain material security. He seems to have been a kindly man, much loved by children. But he too had a short life in front of him, dying of tuberculosis only a year after Ann.

We can, however, gain a clearer picture of Ann's circumstances in the years immediately before her marriage. In 1800 a young woman called Ruth Evans came to live with the family at Dolwar as a kind of servant and companion for Ann. In the same year a young man called John Hughes stayed for some months as a lodger at the farmhouse. John was employed as a teacher in Thomas Charles' circulating schools, and he later became a Methodist minister. A friendship grew up between these three young people which united them, so that for the next few years, until the death of Ann's father, Ruth and John and Ann shared a great many of their deepest thoughts and hopes and aspirations.

It was a special relationship, particularly on account of a fact which we have not yet mentioned. Ann's hymns were, for the most part, never written down in her lifetime. They have come down to us through oral tradition. It

Resurrection's Children

seems that sometimes Ann did write down odd verses on scraps of paper, leaving them behind the cushion on the old chair in the kitchen. But, although both her father and Ruth tried to persuade her to make a fair copy of the hymns, she never would. They were not good enough for that, she thought.

The texts that we have – and they are texts that we rightly rely on – were dictated by Ruth to her husband John Hughes, after Ann's death. Ruth, though able to read, had never learned to write. Consequently we have these incomparable texts written in John Hughes' clumsy handwriting. Ruth had been the singer; it was she who had found the tunes to fit the words which came to Ann. Sometimes, we gather, Ruth also made suggestions for amendments and alterations to the wording.

Although, without any question, the hymns are Ann's, in a strange and rather beautiful way, they are the product of the collaboration of these three people. John was far more widely read in theology than the other two. For one thing, he had quite a good knowledge of English, and he could produce many of the definitions of doctrine which lie behind Ann's verses. Ruth, with her intense but not uncritical admiration for her mistress, was able to encourage and support her in moments of both exultation and despair. And at an early stage it became clear that they were no longer mistress and maid-servant but, as a contemporary says, 'they belonged to a family where both were children of one Father, sisters of one brother, Jesus Christ, to whom they aimed to be faithful in all things'.[7]

John is something of an enigma. All the descriptions of him speak of a man who was clumsy, untidy and ugly, with a harsh voice and an ungracious manner. It may be that there was some actual physical problem in his life; possibly he was spastic. This is nowhere clearly stated, but it seems at least possible. What is sure is that he, like Mary Jones, had come from a very poor family. Like hers, his father had been a weaver who had died when he was a child. There was a great contrast between his clumsiness and Ann's elegance. She loved fine clothes and was conscious of being a leader in the circles in which she moved.

One of the finest of Ann's hymns is devoted entirely to the subject of the Way. Very typically for Ann, it begins where we are, in the perplexities and the disarray of our present life. It begins with the discovery that the Way towards God, as we find it in practice, seems to be directly counter to our fallen nature and its habits. It is only in verses two and three that we realize the full meaning of the hymn, and discover that it is Christ himself who is the Way and that all that is said of the Way in these two verses is really about him. Then the final verse leads us on to meditate on the eternal covenant made before time began in the counsel of the Three-in-One. As H. A. Hodges has commented, 'Thus a meditation on the single word "Way" leads Ann from thoughts of the troubles of her daily life into the eternal counsels of God.'

What does Ann find there at the heart of eternity? She finds the wine of the Kingdom – the new wine which, on the night of his betrayal, Jesus promises to drink with his disciples when he comes into that Kingdom. This is the wine of a feast of fulfilment, a joy which here we can only hint at, a fulfilment of the deepest longing and anguish of the human heart, when death itself has been finally overcome. In these lines Ann repeats the words 'to cheer', just as our translator does; this is the wine which is able to cheer to the uttermost, to cheer the heart of God and man.

Resurrection's Children

Though it crosses human nature,
this perplexing path I trace,
I will travel on it calmly,
while I see your precious face;
take the cross as crown and gladly,
through oppression and dismay,
seek the city of fulfilment,
by the straight, though troubled, Way.

Way so ancient never ageing,
Way whose name is Wonderful;
ever new, without beginning,
Way which saves each dying soul;
Way my spouse and Way my sovereign,
winsome Way, as travellers tell;
Way of holiness, I travel
to my rest beyond the veil.

Way the kite, so keen-eyed, misses,
though it shines with midday light,
light, invisible, untrodden,
only faith perceives the sight,
Way that justifies the godless,
where the dead have life restored;
Way of righteousness for sinners,
peace and favour with the Lord.

Way set up before creation,
then revealed to meet our need,
by the promise made in Eden
which announced the woman's seed;
here the covenant is founded,
here the Three-in-One's design,
here eternal wine to cheer us,
cheer us human and divine.[8]

Companions on the Way

In the manuscript of the hymns it is very striking that, immediately preceding this one, there is a hymn which also ends with the thought of heaven, and of the union and communion of human and divine which is the content of heaven.

> O, eternal rest and rapture,
> when I labour here no more,
> found within that sea of wonders,
> where one never sees a shore;
> coming in to life abundant,
> where the Three-in-One is mine;
> boundless sea to swim for ever;
> One the human and divine![9]

It is said that this particular verse came to Ann one Sunday as she was riding back from Bala after taking part in Holy Communion. In the Welsh original the conjunction of the human and the divine is stated in an even more startling fashion than it is in the English translation. Ann speaks of an abundant, never-ending freedom of entrance into the dwelling-places of the Three-in-One; of water to swim in, not to be passed through; of man in God and God in man. And the last line might just as possibly be translated, 'Man as God and God as man.'

In these verses we are gradually initiated into a sense of the mystery of God in God's own being, the mystery of God Three in One, and the mystery of God's action towards us in the person of Jesus Christ, in whom God and humankind are fully reconciled.

IV

Going further into God's mystery

One of the most remarkable things about these hymns of Ann Griffiths, given so unexpectedly in the little house at Dolwar Fach, is the way in which their form and their content coincide. Ann leads us on from the perplexities of our everyday life into the innermost mystery of eternity, and she does this by leading us from one stage of wonder to another, from one level of mystery to another, by her conscious and skilful use of the paradoxes of the Christian faith. Herbert Hodges, with all the clarity and precision of the philosopher's mind, shows us how she does this, taking us further on and further in. I quote from the essay which he wrote in 1976 for the bicentenary of Ann's birth, one of the very last things which he wrote before his death. Her use of paradox is, he says,

> her way of bringing us into her own state of astonishment at the inherent wonders of the Faith. These wonders can be seen, and Ann sees them, on three distinct levels. First comes wonder in the sense of sheer surprise, and the Christian story is full of surprises which Ann delights to savour and to exhibit to us. But second, wonder may mean a mingling of awe and admiration, such as we feel on contemplating the divine wisdom, love and power. In Addison's phrase, which Wesley borrowed, we are lost in wonder, love and praise. And third, wonder may mean the recognition of a mystery, an incomprehensibility, such as we always find in the long run when we look into the being of God and his actions towards us. Ann is filled with wonder in all these

three senses, even in this life; and heaven to her means living in the midst of a sea of wonders.[10]

All this is something which, here and now, we know only in part, only in reflections and enigmas. But we do already have a real knowledge and experience of it. Ann has a powerful sense that we really participate in the resurrection, even now. For her, as she says in this same hymn, Christians are 'children of the resurrection', already given a foretaste of what shall be hereafter.

Already in this life we know something of the eternity of God. Sometimes, indeed, it may be that we are altogether overwhelmed by a moment of insight and understanding, an anticipation of eternity. Ann, with her outstanding gifts of imagination and intelligence – that questing, probing intelligence which Hodges so appreciated – was sometimes taken out of herself in such moments. Indeed, we know that she was sometimes momentarily disabled from carrying on everyday activities. She would go out to the potato shed to collect some potatoes, and would be found there half an hour later, still wrapped up in prayer and thought.

For most of us, such momentary anticipations of heaven are fleeting and frail indeed. We are more conscious of the 'not yet' of eternal life than the 'already'. And yet, in the words of someone as gifted as Ann was we can recognize truths which awaken echoes within us, truths to which our whole being resonates.

Questions for discussion

1. The friendship between Ann Griffiths, Ruth Evans and John Hughes provided the milieu in which Ann's genius flourished. Have you had experience of the way in which a small group of friends meeting for prayer, study and common activity can build one another up in Christian and human confidence and maturity?

2. Early Methodism, both in England and Wales, was a movement which combined fervent preaching, noisy and exuberant singing and heartfelt services of Holy Communion. Was this combination of evangelical, charismatic and sacramental elements part of the strength of the movement? To what extent do we see these elements being held together in Christian faith and worship today?

3. Have big gatherings for prayer and worship (as at Greenbelt, for instance) been important in your own life? Should there be more such occasions in the life of the churches in Britain?

Chapter 3

The Harvest of Maturity
Waldo Williams

I
Introduction

There are many ways of journeying through life. For some the journey seems to be inward rather than outward. These are the contemplative natures whose gift is to see everything from the beginning, and then to spend the rest of their lives gradually entering into the content of what they saw at the start. Julian of Norwich is a person of this kind. At the age of thirty, in the course of three days, she received her showings of divine love, and then spent the rest of her long life enclosed in her solitary cell beside St Julian's Church in Norwich, constantly travelling further and further in, further into the mysteries of the divine love which had been shown to her in that initial moment of gift and grace.

Among the poets of the mid-century in Welsh-speaking Wales, Waldo Williams was undoubtedly a person of this type. Outwardly his life was not particularly eventful. The son of a school-teacher, he spent most of his life teaching children in primary schools in villages in Wales, and also for some years in England. It was for most of its course an outwardly unremarkable existence. Waldo was a natural contemplative. The experiences and insights of his childhood and adolescence were things which he lived with and wrestled with inwardly from then onwards. His greatest poem was the result of forty years of pondering over an experience of human brotherhood which had come to him 'Between Two Fields' in Pembrokeshire, when he was still a schoolboy.

But Waldo was also a man who lived against the grain of his times, and as a result of this, in his late fifties he twice found himself going to prison on account of his refusal to pay income tax which would have gone towards supporting Britain's part in the Korean wars of the 1950s. Waldo knew that, in conscience, he could not support them.

In the same decade he found himself compelled to enter the world of political action, at least for a time, and to stand as parliamentary candidate for Plaid Cymru in his native Pembrokeshire. Naturally, he was not elected. What is remarkable is that he collected over 2,000 votes, an endorsement of his uncompromising stand which revealed something of the respect and affection in which he was held, at least amongst many of his Welsh-speaking fellow countrymen.[1]

There are many ways in which we might examine Waldo Williams' life and work. In this chapter we will look at two of his later poems. They may seem rather static and show us the consequences of a journey through life rather than the stages of the journey itself. These poems are both elegies, or *marwnadau*, poems written in praise and celebration of someone deeply known and deeply loved, in the moment after their death.[2]

In another context I have suggested that poems such as these, which are written in Welsh in a strict and highly traditional metre and style, have something in common with the Russian and Greek icons of the saints which link

The Harvest of Maturity

people in this life with people in the world to come. They give us a picture of the person concerned as seen in the light of eternity, in the light of God's purposes for them. This is not a detailed, chatty representation of the person. It concentrates on the person's relationship with God, and on the way in which they have been able to mediate that God-ward relationship to their fellow men and women and to the world around them.[3]

The poetry of Waldo Williams is very difficult to translate. In this chapter I am relying on Tony Conran's remarkable book *The Peacemakers* (1997), both for the translations which it contains and for its illuminating introduction and notes. It is a book which has rendered an immense service to readers both in Wales and in England, making this poet, at once so complex and yet so simple, more widely and more easily accessible.

Waldo Williams' friends felt an immense affection for him. He had a total lack of convention, and an almost childlike sense of the ridiculous in life. At the same time people saw in him a painful quality of compassion, a readiness to bear the pain of other people. These things combined to make him a man of a very special character. Speaking at his funeral, his friend James Nicholas described him in terms taken from Russian Orthodoxy:

> I once read of someone asking Berdyaev [one of Waldo's great heroes] 'Do you reckon yourself one of the fools for Christ?' Berdyaev answered 'You don't find their race walking this earth anymore. But I should like to think of myself as one of their descendants.' And this is how I look upon Waldo – one of the descendants of the blessed fools for Christ.[4]

Waldo is a man who makes it more possible, at the end of our frightening century, to feel hope for the human race, and to feel confidence that in the face of all the darkness of our times, the light has still not been overcome. Above all, he is a man who does something to redeem the spiritual mediocrity of our times in this island of Britain.

II

All things rest in love

We have said that Waldo was a natural contemplative. We might also have said that he was a natural mystic. That word 'mystic' has been used and misused in so many ways that it has become almost impossible to use it at all. But let us say that a mystic is one who sees directly what most of us only believe on trust, and that a mystic is one who has a deep and all-embracing sense of the unity of all things in God. Herbert Hodges, whose understanding of Ann Griffiths we have already seen, spent his life as a professional teacher of philosophy and theology. He told me once that as a schoolboy, walking home through Sheffield on a particularly grey and dismal November evening, he heard within himself the words 'All things rest in love', and he felt strangely comforted and affirmed. Indeed, he went on, 'The whole of my life has been the exploration of the meaning of those words.'

Waldo Williams himself was not only a natural mystic, in the sense that he saw directly into the eternal world and glimpsed its oneness; he was also a natural mystic in the particular sense that he saw and experienced this eternal oneness in the world of nature and in the world of the everyday. He had, for instance, a profound conviction of the importance of the dawn – the point where night meets day – as the moment in which the eternal world draws near to the world of time. In his long ode in praise of St David, he sees the dawn of each day as the moment of Jesus' resurrection, the moment when life breaks out of the tomb. The morning star announces Christ's rising, the sun itself brings it to us:

> The morning star that has such lovely power
> is the angel of his great gospel,
> the sun which breaks out from the fetters of the east.
> Through these, everyday, God gives his youth,
> kneel for his sake when he fills the dawn.[5]

For Waldo 'at every break of day the creator's miracle is repeated'. From the hand of the Lord as creator and redeemer alike, there comes the healing light of a simple morning, and Waldo adds, 'what grace could be commoner than that?' This is a theme which we shall later see developed further.

As we read Waldo Williams' work we see how much he sensed the presence of God in the world of nature. Those of us who are active members of a church ought, perhaps, to ask ourselves whether in the past century we have been too critical of those who have claimed to find their way to God outside the walls of church buildings. These two ways of coming to know God's presence need not be mutually exclusive. Evidently they were not for Waldo, and perhaps they need not be for us.

It is interesting to compare Waldo's vision of this moment of dawn with that of a poet in Wales some three centuries earlier, who was also in love with the daily coming of the light:

> Mornings are mysteries; the first world's youth,
> Man's resurrection and the future's bud
> Shroud in their births . . .[6]

Resurrection's Children

There are three things which Henry Vaughan points out to us here as hidden in every dawn: first, the creation, in which God saw all that he had made and beheld that it was very good; secondly, the moment of man's resurrection from sin and death; and thirdly, the anticipation of the future fulfilment of all things. All these are made present to us every day in the coming of the light. What grace could be commoner than that?

Waldo loved to see the presence of God in the most common and everyday things. When he was a boy, Jesus' words about his easy yoke were not a problem to him at all; country people such as he and his parents were well accustomed to carrying pails of water and milk with the help of a yoke on their shoulders. So this simple method of taking the weight of things becomes a way of speaking about the ultimate realities of God's way with men and women. Taking up Christ's words about himself as the Way, the Truth and the Life, and feeling in his body Christ's words about the easy yoke, Waldo writes at the climax of his great ode:

> The way, the life, will not cease
> nor the truth which the soul loves,
> the tree of finest fruit
> the husbandman with the easy yoke.
> His husbandry is in the heart
> and he waits on the rim of our yearning,
> enough for a community and enough
> to yoke together the races throughout the wide world.[7]

That Way, that Truth and that Life can create the true community of neighbourhood in the smallest human groupings, in that sharing of life and work which Waldo knew as a boy and as a young man in his beloved Preseli

The Harvest of Maturity

Hills, a sharing which was made real in all the hardness and limitation of a rural poverty which was sometimes severe. But that same Truth, Way and Life had, he was sure, truly universal implications. It could yoke together all the races of the human family across our world, into a unity of life and shared experience and understanding.

III

Joy and grief are interwoven

We turn now to look at the two poems in which Waldo celebrates two people who were very close to him. The first is his mother Angharad, the second his lifelong friend E. Llwyd Williams.

The first of these two poems is relatively short. Here it is, in Tony Conran's translation. In my commentary I shall sometimes suggest a more literal version of the original and sometimes a simple paraphrase:

> Many by night she worried
> Over, or rejoiced when they did,
> Felt the woe, joined in the feast –
> Those her heart's ocean cherished.
> To her porch all in trouble
> And the feeble knew her hall.
> Angharad's gown of scarlet,
> Woven of deeds, reached her feet.
>
> She bore the care of sufferers
> And with shared strength, cast out fears.
> On her knees in the grey dawn
> Gave her day to the Kingdom,
> Today's simplicity bringing

Resurrection's Children

As wine to the wounded King.
By praising God, over again
To create a world unfallen.
Sister of sun, of the breezes,
Of the day where the wave plays,
Sister to the anxious stars
In the zeal of their musters.

Broke down anger and envy,
Healed with the fruits of her tree,
Broadened the wide gift freely.
Old anguish opened her heart –
A yearning that bore witness
To its deep root in the soil.
She gave to God twofold care,
Both woe and joy together.
To us gave, like the sky of God,
Her anxiety's priesthood.[8]

For many, though she was troubled at night time, yet she rejoiced with them too. From the beginning the poem's theme is announced. We are to be shown the picture of a life which is fulfilled in its fruitful holding together of two things essential to human living – joy and sorrow, happiness and anxiety. Waldo's mother is a person who feels the pain of her fellow human beings and yet also rejoices in their feast. In the ocean of her heart there is cherishing. The human heart, as Christopher Fry says, can go to the lengths of God. Its capacities are unfathomable, oceanic. The reference to Angharad's scarlet gown is a reference to a well-known medieval poem in praise of a noble lady who was clothed in scarlet. The gown of Waldo's Angharad is woven of good deeds.

In her capacity as the wife of the head-teacher of the primary school, she becomes the confidante of many. She

The Harvest of Maturity

takes the cares of others, and by sharing their cares and their fears she is able to share with them her strength. For her, as for her son, the grey dawn was the vital moment of the day. She gave the simplicity of her day to the King and to the wound. Here it is Christ the King who has become the wounded man lying by the wayside. In the simplicity of her offered gift, Angharad, like the good Samaritan, pours wine and oil into his wounds, which are the world's wounds. In the simplicity of her praise, which is his praise, she recreates an unblemished world.

The whole of the praise tradition in Welsh poetry, which has been at work for more than a thousand years, has as its end and purpose to give back to us 'the clear unfallen world'. And Angharad's work of listening and sympathizing, encouraging and strengthening, is all done in the energy which comes from this time in the grey dawn, this time on her knees, this time of prayer and praise. And all this, which is hidden in the privacy of the school-teacher's house, in the triviality of everyday life in the small village, is something of universal and cosmic significance. It is precisely not something cramped and turned in on itself. It is the result of a life lived in harmony with the movements of the winds and the waves, of the sun and the stars. The whole universe is moved in this rhythm of joy and sorrow, of play and delight, of care and zealous concern.

So, in the ripeness of her age, in which the two movements have come together into one, she is able to break down anger and envy, healing with the fruits of her tree. She is able to broaden out the wide gift freely. The immemorial yearning of the human heart – that yearning which is rooted in the deepest place of our humanity – has opened out in her to receive all who come.

So she gave to God her life in both its aspects, joy and grief in harmony. She gives to us, with the wide inclusiveness of God's heaven, the priesthood of her concern, *offeiriadaeth ei phryder*. The word which Tony Conran translates as 'anxiety' – it might also be translated 'trouble' – seems to me at this point to be most suitably rendered by the word 'concern'. This is particularly the case when we take that word with its Quaker connotation of a task, a responsibility – sometimes an anxious task, a heavy responsibility, taken on behalf of others. So Angharad stretches out her loving concern, her prayer of intercession, over the life of her village world, which is a microcosm of our whole world.

There is an echo here, probably but not certainly unconscious, of the Byzantine image of the protecting veil of prayer which the mother of God spreads out over the city of Constantinople. This is an image which has long been pictured for us in the icons of the Eastern Church, and which is now made present in a new way, in the music of one of the most widely known of all John Tavener's compositions, the work for cello and orchestra called *The Protecting Veil of the Mother of God*.

IV

The harvest of understanding and goodwill

The Welsh original of this poem, 'Angharad', is included in Waldo's one published collection called *Dail Pren, The Leaves of the Tree*, which appeared in 1956. It is written in the metre and style of a medieval *cywydd*. In the last period of his life Waldo was more and more drawn to employ this traditional form, which is still often used by 'country poets' for poems of praise and congratulation. These are poems which, as Tony Conran says, are not

The Harvest of Maturity

'about someone or something or an idea, but are to a specific person at a specific time for a specific reason.'

So, for instance, in 1959 Waldo writes a *cywydd* in praise of his old friend W. R. Evans, on the occasion of his retiring as headmaster of the school at Bwlch-y-Groes. In 1961 he writes a *cywydd* of thanks to a fellow poet, Isfoel, for the gift of a thumbstick, and he also writes a particularly joyful poem of congratulation addressed to Mr and Mrs Tommy James of Ysgeifiog near Solfa on the occasion of their golden wedding anniversary. The bridegroom, James Nicholas tells us, was a clog-maker. He had lived his whole life in Ysgeifiog, in a thoroughly Welsh-speaking community. He also had a strong sense of humour, which is reflected in the poem, which at one moment breaks into six lines of English.[9] In 1964 there is a similarly exuberant *cywydd* of praise with a more public figure in view – D. J. Williams, perhaps the most popular of all the personalities involved in the early leadership of Plaid Cymru.

It is in the context of these late poems that we need to seek the work which we shall examine next. It is in some ways a more solemn and a more complex poem than them, for it was written in 1960 after the death of E. Llwyd Williams. As well as being a close friend with whom Waldo had published jointly a collection of children's poems in 1936, Llwyd had been for many years the Baptist minister at Rhydaman.

This is a work which, like 'Angharad', seeks to give a total picture or icon of the person concerned at the time of their death; an icon of the person seen in the light of God. But here the picture is more detailed, and Waldo celebrates someone who is both a poet and a minister of Christ. If, in the case of 'Angharad', there had been a union of joy and grief in the maturity of her life, here we see

Resurrection's Children

another image of human fulfilment in the conjunction of the pastoral work of the active minister with the inward vision of the poet and the man of prayer.

In these lines we discover again how the sharp particularity of a poem written for 'a specific person at a specific time for a specific reason' makes possible a powerful statement of a truly universal vision and understanding of our human calling to live our life for God and in God.

> If Llwyd's dead, what's all language?
> No sentence more than a dream.
> A cold mist on a bare moor,
> If meaning's lost between us.
> Pure God, father of light, bring
> Back to us your bright dawning.
> Your glory is your heart. Love shoots
> From you, up from the saint root.
> Your love's tied above our clay,
> Knots over fall a safe stay.
> In our severance dwell, so we
> Into one House may journey![10]

The poem begins from an acute sense of loss, and a sense that the death of the poet – the 'maker', as it would have been in medieval English – involves a threat to the whole language and to all meaning. It may be difficult, in an English context, to feel the full weight of this sense of bereavement. The English language is spoken and written in so many places – some of its greatest poets are found as far away as Australia or the West Indies – that we are not so acutely aware of the loss involved in the death of an individual writer. But in the case of a language whose very existence is under threat, the death of a scholar – above all, the death of a poet – is something desolating. It seems to strike at the very possibility of maintaining the

The Harvest of Maturity

coherence and vitality of a living tradition of understanding, communication and interchange.

The loss of language implicit in the poet's death is felt as a 'cold mist on a barren moor', and at once, in the face of the darkness an appeal is made to God as the Father of light, to give us back the dawn. We have already seen the significance of the dawn to Waldo, as a moment of new creation and a moment of resurrection. Here he calls upon God's love, which is his glory, to dawn upon us, to bind us together 'above our clay', to keep us united even in the moment of the separation which death brings, and then to bring us together on our final journey into the one house of heaven.

In the next two passages of the poem Waldo celebrates his friend, above all, as the pastor of his congregation, a shepherd of Christ's people, a steward of the mysteries of God:

> My brother, to me faultless,
> His blessing was gentleness,
> Llwyd, good night! Oh how meek,
> How rich, how modest he was!
> And the sap of the vine still
> Flowed in him, a sure goodwill.
> Open and mild amongst us, unlost
> He carried home the harvest.
>
> Shepherd, with his honest face,
> In Rhydaman a long space
> (Good steward) tried to see sense,
> Bring hearts into God's presence,
> The unfailing fullness, God's
> Husbandry of neighbourhood.

Resurrection's Children

Congregations of all kinds, perhaps particularly small-town congregations, can be centres of misunderstanding, bickering and small-scale back-biting. This shepherd has been one who, by his own gentle attentiveness to all, has helped people to be open and attentive to one another. In his daily, undramatic work as a pastor, he has gathered a people together into an eternal harvest – 'God's husbandry of neighbourhood'.

The stress put on Llwyd's gentleness, modesty and kindness – or, to use the Gospel term, his meekness – is very striking in this passage. This poem was written almost forty years ago, when our society was much less violent than it is today. There seems to be something prophetic in it here. The need for gentleness is even more striking now than it would have been then. It is instructive to see how, in a situation like ours, with its 'physical violence, verbal violence, economic violence, structural and institutional violence, spiritual violence ... intensified by its being vividly represented in the media so that violence often dominates imaginations', a theologian of the calibre of David Ford can stress the irreplaceable value of gentleness in building up the life of our society.[11]

It would be interesting to enquire why it was that in the Welsh Nonconformity of forty years ago this quality of gentleness seems to have been so highly prized and so carefully cultivated. Was it in reaction against a certain kind of ministry which had tried to affirm its authority by shouting too loudly, both literally and metaphorically? Was it in the face of a certain tendency to exploit human emotions too quickly in the service of the gospel? Whatever its sources were, such a controlled and deeply felt gentleness as described here can be, in our violent time, an impressive counter-sign and one of the greatest importance.

This gentleness is significant above all in that it seeks to

The Harvest of Maturity

bring about that personal recognition and understanding between people which Waldo so greatly valued. The exigencies of the rhyme here show Llwyd, in Conran's translation, as 'seeking to see sense'. In the original it is understanding he is seeking – seeking to lead the one into the confidence of the other, to help them to understand one another and thus to bring the whole congregation into the harvesting of God.

> My cry of loss on flecked floor,
> Llwyd, hid bard of Allt Cilau-fawr.
> On phantoms light has broken,
> Its genius has left the sun.
> And from his home and threshold
> The dear man left Wythcae's world –
> Gave up walking the hill brim
> For two yards in Rhydwilym.
> Oh, where's vision, free created?
> A great wound is a poet's death.
> Raise our race, keep our folk hoard,
> Lift your burden on us, Lord,
> And for the three dear ones, turn
> Mist at the ford to sunshine.

If the previous lines stressed Llwyd's work as a minister of Christ's Church, the lines which follow have a sharper, more anguished tone, as Waldo thinks of him again directly as a friend and fellow poet. 'A great wound is a poet's death.' Here again the image of a cold, enveloping mist is contrasted with the light of God, a glimpse of the sun which breaks through the murk and the darkness bringing warmth and illumination. In his comment on this poem Tony Conran reminds us that something very remarkable is taking place in these lines, with their epigrammatic conciseness, packing much into a little space – a quality which

Resurrection's Children

is common in classical Welsh verse. There is here a fusion of the old and the new, the individual and the universal. Conran writes, 'It is the enormity of his key changes, modulating from the dead man to God, to poetry, to the land, and finally to the three bereaved ones [Llwyd's widow and two daughters], all within about six or seven lines, that is so extraordinary.'[12]

We see clearly how the universal and the particular come very close together in these lines. We pass from the observation of the dear man leaving his house for two yards in the graveyard in Rhydwilym to the point where we mourn the loss of the free, creative imagination and declare that the poet's death is the loss of a whole people. But in the end we find light through our darkness, light in our darkness.

> Let me greet you, good soul. Glinted
> Light breaks through the vale of dread.
> I keep your balm for always,
> Preaching, that tips summer days
> To sing forever. 'Blessed
> Are the meek.' A glitter, a glad
> Preaching a nightingale's tune –
> The grove of night's full heaven.
> Your music is there. Shine, and
> Spread its gift over the land.

In the last paragraph of the poem themes and images from earlier on are gathered together. A kind of resolution is brought to the disarray of the previous section. Light does break through into the valley of the shadow of death. The memory of the one who has died is full of healing balm; summer returns with the thought of his message, 'Blessed are the meek.' This is a message which, as we have seen, he had conveyed not only with his words but by his whole life and way of being. Literally translated, the following

The Harvest of Maturity

lines read: 'A green world of bright preaching, pure song of the nightingale.' We do not expect the preaching of a Baptist chapel to be compared with the woodland song of the nightingale. We are in a different world here from England and America.

Here, as Conran points out, Waldo is referring to a famous poem by the nineteenth-century writer Alun, in which the poet makes the nightingale with its song a symbol of the devoted wife comforting her husband after the distresses of the day. Thus, in her self-sacrifice, she prefigures the hope of the dawn, the possibility of new creation. It is an image which R. S. Thomas has used to great effect in one of his finest poems to his first wife.

In these lines the image suggests that the life and teaching of the Baptist minister have themselves become a work of self-sacrificing love, filling the darkness of our night, our sense of loss, with a music as healing as that of the nightingale. The grove of night is full of heaven; the stars are there and bring their light, which accompanies the song of the poet, the preaching of the pastor. May God's light shine out, may the gift of his grace spread over the land. It is a remarkable conclusion to a striking and unexpected poem, full of a surprising power of healing and life. Tony Conran remarks about this poem:

> it involves you in experiencing the dead man's life, not just as a pattern of moral goodness but as a sacrament, a renewal of grace. The poem remembers and re-activates in us God's love that flowed through Llwyd when he was alive. The death-defying quality of art celebrates the victory over death of the community of saints in Christ.[13]

Ann Griffiths, whose love of paradox we have already noted, in one verse describes the Christian life with a wonderful triple paradox: 'I shall walk slowly all my days under the shadow of the cross, and as I walk I shall run, and as I run I shall stand still and see the peace which will be mine when I come to rest beyond the grave.'[14] Waldo, as we said earlier, was a natural contemplative, one who loved to stand still and gaze into the things of eternity. In the course of our studies in this book we have been thinking of the Christian life as a journey – a journey through this world of space and time, but also a journey from this world into the great world which lasts for ever.

In this chapter we have paused for a moment in front of two icons of lives which outwardly were not particularly adventurous or journeying – the wife of a village schoolmaster and the minister of a Baptist chapel in a small country town. Inwardly, however, they were lives which had travelled far, in which inner and outer, personal and public themes had been linked together, for they were lives which, even if they were lived on a small stage, were nonetheless lived under a public gaze. Through their daily offering of their lives to God, both Angharad and Llwyd had arrived at a certain wholeness and maturity. This is a wholeness or integration which comes about when people are willing to bring together within themselves different aspects of human experience, and thus are able to become for the world in which they live people who, in small and outwardly insignificant ways, can promote peace and reconciliation. So their lives can show us, even in this world, some corner of the light and gentleness of the world to come.

The Harvest of Maturity

Questions for discussion

1. Following the old Welsh tradition of praise poetry, Waldo Williams praises his mother and his friend. Do we sufficiently appreciate and value the gifts of God in other people? Try writing a 'praise poem' for someone who has been important in your own life and has helped you to see something of the goodness of God and the grace of Jesus Christ.

2. Differences of outlook, temperament and background can easily lead to misunderstanding and dissension. On the other hand, such differences can be a source of great enrichment if we learn to appreciate those who are different from ourselves. Are we willing and able to learn from people who differ from us? Are we confident enough to listen to what they are saying, even when we disagree?

3. Waldo and Gwenallt found themselves at odds with society in Britain and were ready to go to prison for conscience's sake. To what extent are we ready to recognize the call of particular individuals to go against the consensus of their times? What do we think of those who protest today over Green issues or questions of war and peace? What do we make of the Quaker peace testimony? Have you had personal contact with members of a Quaker meeting?

Chapter 4

On the Roads of Wales
D. Gwenallt Jones

I
Introduction

David James Jones (but we shall call him by his bardic name, Gwenallt) was born in 1899. He grew up in Pontardawe, an industrial district to the north of Swansea. His family background was solidly working class and intensely Methodist; in the first years of his life the chapel had an all-pervasive influence on him. Gwenallt's father, who worked in the local steel works, was not only a deacon in the chapel, but was also a well-known local poet. Gwenallt had his first lessons in poetry from him.

Already, in his boyhood, Gwenallt was aware of the tensions and conflicts in capitalist society, as experienced from beneath. For instance, there was the violence of strikes and lock-outs. These early experiences of working-class solidarity, of resentment against the employers and of the close-knit fellowship of the chapel community were with him all his life. For some years he rejected the Christian faith he had grown up with, but when it came back to him, albeit in a somewhat altered form, he knew that it was the same faith that he was rediscovering, something which had been with him from the beginning.[1]

As a writer Gwenallt made a very deep impression on

at least two readers in England who had taken the trouble to learn Welsh. It is not surprising that Herbert Hodges, whom we have already encountered, should have felt a particular affinity for his work. He too had grown up in a working-class milieu, in a Methodist family in Sheffield. He too had passed through a period of agnosticism before he rediscovered his faith in a Catholic Anglican form. It is Hodges' translations of Gwenallt's poetry which we shall be using throughout this chapter.[2]

Another lay theologian who was a great lover of Gwenallt was Donald Nicholl, the Roman Catholic teacher and prophet of more recent years. In the upstairs study of his house, where in the last months of his life he had his bed, Donald put on the bookshelves small pictures of his particular friends and companions on the way towards God. There was the nineteenth-century Russian monk, Seraphim of Sarov; the French hermit of the Sahara, Charles de Foucauld; David Jones, the Anglo-Welsh painter and poet; Thich Nhat Hanh, the Buddhist monk from Vietnam who made such a direct contact with Thomas Merton; the German-Jewish philosopher and Carmelite nun, Edith Stein, whose work Donald had translated when he was young, and who died a martyr in a Nazi concentration camp.

In the midst of this wonderfully diverse company, there was a photograph of Gwenallt, one of a number of pictures taken during the last months of his life, when the cancer which was to kill him had already marked his face. It is a face which shows an extraordinary mingling of joy and sadness, of serenity and pain. You have only to read the opening pages of Donald Nicholl's book, *The Testing of Hearts*, with its moving description of the last days of his own father's life, to realize how close his sense of identification with Gwenallt would have been. Donald Nicholl too had grown up in all the poverty and hardship of a Pennine pit village. He too had seen England in the thirties from below, and had never forgotten what it looked like. Like Gwenallt, he had known all the wealth of human life which can be hidden in such surroundings.[3]

There was something wonderfully true and yet unexpected in Donald's placing Gwenallt there in the midst of such a resolutely international and ecumenical company. They are all people whose lives have reflected, and at times have helped to shape, some of the deeper currents of the history of the twentieth century. This is the kind of wide context in which Gwenallt needs to be seen. In terms of Europe in particular, Gwenallt had a remarkably ecumenical vision: the north, the south, the east – all have their place for him. Protestants, Catholics, Orthodox – all have given their martyrs in our time, both for their faith and for human freedom, in the face of the totalitarian barbarism both of the Left and the Right. As Herbert Hodges wrote:

> Gwenallt's writings come straight up out of the tensions of the society around him, which were fought out vividly in his own soul; between the rural culture of Wales and industrialism, between Wales and England, nationalism and imperialism, pacifism and passionate revolt, Christianity and Marxism, socialist theory and the actualities of human life,

His writings 'come straight up'; yes, they bubble up like molten lava from a volcano. Sometimes one feels that the poems were written too quickly, that perhaps the writer should have reflected on them longer before he committed them so passionately to paper. Yet, such was the nature of the man. If his work at times lacks finish, at times it gains greatly by a vivid immediacy all its own.

If we compare him with Waldo Williams, we should have to say that his journey through life, his journey of faith, was more stormy, and more directly involved in the problems of society than Waldo's had been. It was only in 1960 and again in 1961, when he was in his late fifties, that Waldo found himself in prison for conscience's sake, and then his sentences were brief and were served in the comparatively humane conditions of an open prison.

Gwenallt was still in his teens when he went to prison for two years in 1917 for refusing military service. He spent those years in two of the most brutal establishments in the British penal system, Wormwood Scrubs and Dartmoor. His objection to military service was at least as much political as religious: he was already deeply influenced by Marxism and was greatly impressed by the leaders of the Easter Rising in Dublin in 1916. Christian pacifism, international socialism and Welsh nationalism were all factors in his refusal to enlist.[4]

However different their temperaments and however different the circumstances of their imprisonment, it is important to reflect on the fact that both these deeply Christian and deeply thoughtful men, Gwenallt and Waldo, found themselves unable in conscience to accept the authority of the British state – a state which, indeed, they were unable to recognize as their own.

II

The redemption of the body

In Gwenallt's 1959 collection of poems, *Gwreiddiau (Roots)*, there is a poem called 'A Changed World'. It gives us a first impression of how he saw his journey from the

Resurrection's Children

optimistic rationalism of his youth to the mature convictions which he held in the 1940s. The poet moves from a naïve belief in progress, embraced in his schoolboy revolt against the Methodist world of his childhood, to the rediscovered faith which supported him through the anxieties of the early years of the Cold War. It was a time when the prospect of a worldwide nuclear contest sometimes seemed perilously near.

> I got a glimpse of that sunny world
> Before the First World War;
> I saw that mankind had left the Egypt
> Of poverty, captivity and the Christian superstitions;
> Mankind had made its way through the wilderness of
>   the middle ages,
> And under the sun of the revival of learning
> Was marching in procession, jaunty and fine, over
>   stream and hill,
> Gaining in knowledge, comfort and justice.
> I went to the top of Nebo
> To take a glance at Canaan, perfect in equality, justice
>   and welfare;
> And the future before us was an unending triumph on
>   earth.
>
> What a gulf there is between that world and our
>   world
> After two world wars!
> Canaan has vanished like the magic mist in the
>   Mabinogion,
> And Nebo was nothing but a volcano
> Blowing out its entrails into the wind.
> Our modern world, according to some,
> Is just a meaningless waste;

And the old Christian superstitions have come back
   again,
Superstitions like the end of the world,
'End of the world and day of judgement' . . . .[5]

For some at that time – Gwenallt had in view some of the early existentialists – the modern world was seen as a desert empty of all meaning. For others it had become a place in which it was possible, indeed indispensable, to rediscover Christianity and to see it afresh. In a fascinating autobiographical essay called *I Believe*, published in 1943, Gwenallt gives us an account of how he did this. As well as telling us how his mind had developed during the inter-War years, this essay also shows us how he saw the Christian faith by 1943.

1943 was a year of some significance for him: it was in that year that he decided that if he was to be a Christian at all, he had to be a member of a church. But here he faced a problem. He felt then that he could not go back to Calvinistic Methodism. He did not feel able to take the road that leads to Rome. He decided to be confirmed in the Church in Wales, and began to worship regularly in the historic parish church of Llanbadarn Fawr, near Aberystwyth, where he was teaching in the university.

The vision of Christianity which is expressed in this essay, and still more in the poetry of the next two decades, has many distinctly Catholic characteristics. It is a vision which has a strong sense of the historic continuity of the Church through the ages. For Gwenallt, as a student and teacher of Welsh literature, as well as a poet of distinction, this continuity is seen as something embodied not only in the Church's faith and worship, but also in the underlying continuities of the Welsh tradition, with its strong Christian pre-suppositions. Of course, there were contrasts –

Resurrection's Children

sometimes very strong ones – within this tradition. For instance, there was the contrast between the strongly affirmative vision of the medieval poet, Dafydd ap Gwilym, and the other-worldly emphasis of the eighteenth-century hymn-writer Pantycelyn. But Gwenallt sees them as contrasting figures within a single tradition. There is continuity as well as discontinuity between the pre-Reformation and the post-Reformation centuries. This tradition is something which can contain both.

Gwenallt's sense of the unity of the Church through time was complemented and reinforced by his strong sense of the communion of saints in heaven and on earth, his sense that the Church now and the Church of previous times are in reality one. For, as Pavel Florensky, a Russian theologian of our own century, loved to say, 'The past has not passed away.' In the power of the Holy Spirit, the Church on earth and the Church in heaven are united across the barrier of death; it is this faith which finds full expression in Gwenallt's poem on St David, as we shall see later.

This newly gained sense of the Church, as at once a reality of time and a reality of eternity, brings us to another aspect of Gwenallt's understanding of the Christian faith as we find it in his mature writings. This is its all-embracing quality. For him, Christianity is not primarily a religion of either/or. It is a religion of both/and. Looking back at the evangelical religion of his childhood, it seemed to him to have been in some ways dangerously one-sided. It seemed to say that to love God, even to believe in him, we had to turn our backs on the world that he had created.

Gwenallt was now sure that before Christianity could safely be world-denying, it needed to be world-affirming. God had made both flesh and spirit so he must be found through both. So, in one of the most powerful of his sonnets, he declares:

> God has not forbidden us to love the world,
> And to love man and all his works,
> To love them with all the naked senses,
> Every shape and colour, every voice and every speech;
> There is a shudder in our blood when we see the trace
> Of his craftsman's hands upon the round creation,
> And a ferment, when we cry out in mad triumph
> That we do not want a life like this life.
> And when the spirit leaves the robe of flesh
> Folded stiff and cold in the coffin,
> Surely it will come some time on its journey,
> To put it on again like a robe of honour;
> To take to itself the body, nostrils, sight and hearing,
> To make sensuous the glories of God.[6]

In such a vision of things, we are drawn to go beyond this world, to long for a life which is *not* like this life, by the very strength and vehemence of our love for this world, in all its infinite variety, beauty and strangeness. It is through the things of this world that we are called to look beyond this world. For this is a world which God has made, and in its very stuff we can see the traces of his skilful craftsman's hands. These traces make us long to enter into a personal relation with the one who is responsible for them. We remember that Irenaeus, one of the greatest of all the early Christian theologians, says, 'It is through his two hands of love, the Son, and the Spirit, that the Father makes the world.'

Of this particular poem we may say that it shows not only a deeply Catholic sense of the holiness of the material world, but also a very specific understanding of the significance of our faith in the resurrection of the body. It is in and with the body that is to be raised that we catch a glimpse of the restoration of the whole of creation. Here Gwenallt takes up an idea which is very dear to the early

Resurrection's Children

Christian writers both of Wales and of Ireland; something which may truly be called characteristic of the early Celtic centuries of our islands. It is also the theme of some of the greatest theologians of the Christian East.

In such a way of seeing things it is not difficult to see the world itself as a sacrament of God's wisdom and love, and to see the sacramental rite which lies at the heart of the Church's life as a rite of universal and cosmic significance. For the Eucharist is seen not only as the memorial of Christ's death, as the early Methodists had often tended to do, following the one-sided emphasis to be found in the Prayerbook rite of Archbishop Cranmer. In the celebration of the Eucharist we find that the whole mystery of Christ is made present: incarnation, transfiguration, ascension, Pentecost – all are there, gathered around the mid-most point of death and resurrection.

Gwenallt expresses something of this all-inclusiveness of the mystery of Christ in the essay of 1943:

> Christianity is the fellowship of the crib, the fellowship of the transfiguration, the fellowship of the last supper, of the garden, the cross, the resurrection, the ascension and the second coming. The three things essential to the gospel are the crib, the cross and the empty tomb. We can look at the two pieces of the cross, the vertical piece is like an image of the relationship between God and man, man down below as a sinner, and God above him as the loving Father, and the horizontal piece is the relationship between man and man, half of it an image of the sciences and half of the arts, and the wounded body holding together the two pieces in one cross. But the meaning of the cross depends on faith in the resurrection. It was in the light of the resurrection that St Paul and the Apostles interpreted the cross.[7]

On the Roads of Wales

In Gwenallt's thinking there is no separation between Good Friday and Easter Day.

III

The gypsy of God

In the light of such affirmations, we can go on to look at one of the finest and most characteristic of all Gwenallt's poems, 'St David'.

> There is no frontier between two worlds in the
>   Church;
> The Church militant upon earth is the same
> As the Church triumphant in heaven.
> And the saints are in this Church which is two in one.
> They come to worship with us, our small
>   congregation,
> The saints, our oldest ancestors,
> Who built Wales on the foundation
> Of the Cradle, the Cross and the Empty Tomb;
> And they go out from it as of old to tread their
>   customary ways
> And to evangelise Wales.

This is the foundation – the presence with us now of the mystery of Christ and the Spirit, in and through the witness and message of the saints. Bethlehem, Jerusalem and Galilee are discovered to be near through the faith and prayer of the servants of Christ, the faith and prayer of those who, now as then, go out to bring the good news to the whole of human society.

> I have seen David going from county to county like God's gypsy
> With the Gospel and the Altar in his caravan;
> And he came to us in the Colleges and schools
> To show us what is the purpose of learning.
> He went down to the bottom of the pit with the miners
> And cast the light of his wise lamp onto the coal face;
> At the steel works he put on the spectacles and the short grey overall
> And showed the Christian being purified like the metal in the furnace;
> And he led the industrial people to his disreputable Church.

In his mature writings Gwenallt is always anxious to present us with the possibility and necessity of a Christian humanism. Religion is not something on its own; it exists for the sake of humanity. So the gospel is not a substitute for learning – it is its pre-supposition; it is not a substitute for industry and commerce – it shows us their true purpose and meaning. He expresses his belief in these possibilities in his essay *I Believe*:

> True humanism with God at its centre, allows room for reason and understanding as well as faith, for the beauty of nature, for the arts and sciences, and for co-operation between man and God.

In the line which speaks about the Christian being purified like metal in the furnace, there is a discreet reference to the death of Gwenallt's father, who was killed in 1927 at the age of sixty in a hideous industrial accident involving a fall of molten metal. The preacher's attempts at consolation in his sermon at Gwenallt's father's funeral provoked Gwenallt to one of his most notable outbursts of protest against conventional piety:

> When, in the funeral sermon, the minister said that it was God's will, I cursed his sermon and his God with all the haulier's swear words that I knew, and when they sang the graveside hymn I sang in my heart the 'Red Flag'. If I could, I would have lifted the coffin up out of the grave and shattered the obscene capitalist system that placed more value on production than on life, on profits than on humankind.

The poem continues with these lines:

> He carried his Church everywhere
> Like a body, having life, mind and will
> Doing things small and great.
> He brought the Church into our homes,
> Put the Sacred Vessels on the kitchen table,
> And took bread from the pantry and cheap wine from the cellar,
> And stood behind the table like a tramp
> So as not to hide from us the wonder of the sacrifice.

This poem was published in a collection which appeared in 1951. These lines give a remarkable instance of the quickness with which Gwenallt grasped signs of new life within the church which he had so recently joined. The practice of celebrating the Eucharist in people's homes (House Communions) was, in the years after 1945, something very new amongst Anglicans, whether in England or in Wales. Moreover, at that time for a priest to celebrate the sacrament 'facing the people' in church was scarcely thought of; indeed, it was very seldom possible, since the altar was nearly always placed against the east wall.

But here, in the domestic setting, the priest carefully

stands behind the table, 'so as not to hide from us the wonder of the sacrifice'. All this was being done (where it was being done, and that was not in many places) with a desire to do exactly what Gwenallt's David is doing. He is bringing the Church closer to the people, breaking down the gulf which has opened up between the clergy (not only of one church but of many) and ordinary people, particularly working-class people.

> And after the Communion we had a talk round the fire,
> And he spoke to us of God's natural Order,
> The person, the family, the nation and the society of nations,
> And the Cross which keeps us from turning any of them into a god.
> He said that God has fashioned our nation
> For his own purpose,
> And its death would be a breach of that Order.

Here, after the sacrament has been celebrated (and tea has been drunk too?), the apostle begins to expound the meaning of what has been done. He speaks of God's natural Order, 'The person, the family, the nation and the society of nations, And the Cross which keeps us from turning any of them into a god.' All human institutions, all our human righteousness, stand under the judgement of the cross. In the light which comes from that place, we may be saved from making an idol of any of these things, we may be enabled to see them in their own proper proportion and perspective.

We see how carefully Gwenallt, now the convinced nationalist, situates the nation between the family and the society of nations, both having their own rights. The nationalism of Plaid Cymru, the Welsh Nationalist Party,

On the Roads of Wales

as it had been first formulated by Saunders Lewis in 1930, had always been a resolutely international nationalism. The rights of each nation, no less than the rights of each person, can best be served by caring for the rights of other nations, of other persons.

When this poem has been printed in anthologies in English, as has happened once or twice, it has been usual to end it here. But Gwenallt did not end it here. He went on:

> Anger came to his forehead
> As he lashed us for licking the arse of the Saxon Leviathan,
> And allowing ourselves, in his Christian country,
> To be turned into Pavlov's dogs.
> We besought his pardon, his strength and his keenness,
> And told him, before he left us,
> To give the Lord Jesus Christ our poor congratulations,
> And to ask Him whether we might come to him
> To praise him for ever in Heaven,
> When comes that longed-for moment
> That we have to say Good Night to the world.[8]

Physically Gwenallt was a small man. Like some other short, slight people, he liked to shock and to startle. He had a mischievous and satirical sense of humour; he knew that the poetry of praise needs the poetry of satire to complement it. The Lord Jesus Christ, in the days of his flesh, had driven the money-changers out of the temple with a small whip. Here his saint uses his words to chastise a people whom he feels have become slack, cowardly and indifferent. This was almost half a century ago. What would he say to us now, whether in Wales, England, Scotland or Ireland – what would he say to us today?

IV

Through martyrdom the Kingdom draws near

We have, of course, only begun to tap the riches which are there in the writing of Gwenallt. He was a poet who wrote much and who ranged over many themes. One is the contrast between the world of the countryside on the one hand and the world of the industrial south on the other. Both worlds – the worlds of country and town – have changed beyond recognition in the thirty years since his death. Perhaps Gwenallt is at his most prophetic in relation to the world of the country, where he seems to have had an intuition of some of the issues which we associate with the word 'ecology', long before that word was in common usage.

Another theme to which he keeps returning is that of the proper place of the mind and its activity in the life of faith and in the life of human society. So, in a notable poem addressed to the Bangor theologian J. E. Daniel, he sees the scholar as constructing three rooms in his house: the room devoted to theology, built on foundations laid by the Reformers and the first Fathers of the Church; the room devoted to the classical world of Greece and Rome, 'the cradle of Europe's civilization'; and the room devoted to the history, literature and language of Wales. And he insists that all three rooms are related to one another and belong together – Jerusalem and Athens and Bangor.

This cultural concern is not only related to the study of the past. Gwenallt was vividly aware, before many others were, of the role of the writers of continental Europe – and especially those of Eastern Europe – in keeping the flame of freedom alive in the face of totalitarian oppression.

This is 'the flame of freedom and justice and nationality', 'kindled by the human genius of Greece', yet with its roots in the revelation of God himself.

> The flame that comes from the candles of the last supper in the upper room
> Its light is the light of Eastern morning
> And upon its wick the fiery tongues of Pentecost are speaking.[9]

Already, at the very beginning of the period of the Cold War, Gwenallt saw vividly the role of the writers of the countries in the Soviet bloc, 'whose poetry', as Seamus Heaney was to write towards the end of that Cold War period, 'not only witnesses the poet's refusal to lose his or her cultural memory, but also testifies thereby to the continuing efficacy of poetry itself as a necessary and fundamental human act'. Heaney, no less than Gwenallt, sees this witness as a matter of life and death. He speaks in terms of 'a modern martyrology, a record of courage and sacrifice which elicits our unstinted admiration'.[10]

We have said that there was something Catholic about Gwenallt's approach to Christianity. Was he attracted to Rome? Surely, at times, he was; he was certainly attracted by some of the saints of Latin Catholicism, particularly the Carmelites of Spain, St Teresa and St John of the Cross. But he was troubled by the authoritarianism of Rome as he saw it in the days before Vatican II, and by its apparent preference for uniformity. Herbert Hodges sums it up briefly: 'He thought the Pope was too like a Roman Emperor, and he was not going to fight one imperialism [Marxism] only to sit down under another.'

In the 1950s Gwenallt went to Cyprus for a holiday, and for the first time came into direct contact with the Eastern Churches. He was impressed by their stress on the resurrection. He was impressed too by the way in which the life of the Church seemed to penetrate into the life of ordinary people. He was also pleased to see that the bishops of the Church gave their blessing to the struggle for national independence.

His poem about Cyprus is not one of his greatest, but the image of the light of Easter, being carried from the altar into every part of the society of the place, is powerfully realized:

> From the light behind the altar every candle is lighted,
> And it is carried to re-kindle the candle on every hearth,
> And to re-illuminate street, square, vineyard and cemetery,
> Until the town is a sea of candles,
> And the land is alive with the dawn of Easter.[11]

In this chapter we have seen the way in which Gwenallt's own journey through life involved him in many of the major cultural and political issues of his day, and in the end, in the deepest issue of all – our relationship with God. His life was certainly not always tranquil, not always without complications. Having found his way into the Anglican tradition in 1944, thirteen years later he felt compelled to leave the Anglican Communion on account of what seemed to him – not without justification at the time – to be a lack of concern for the Welsh tradition and all that it stood for. He returned to the Calvinistic Methodism of his youth, and became a loyal member of the Tabernacle Chapel in Aberystwyth.

Judging by his poetry, while this return to his roots deepened his sense of indebtedness to the hymns which he had learnt in his childhood, and while it renewed his Evangelical convictions, it certainly did not alter the Catholic elements in his mature position. He continued to explore the Evangelical-Catholic direction of his thought – a direction which I believe has greater ecumenical significance today than has commonly been recognized.[12]

In his poem on St David he sees the saint journeying throughout the counties of Wales, through town and country, and taking us with him. But the poem begins with the journey to eternity, asserting that there is no barrier between heaven and earth in the Church, and it ends with the thought of that moment which each one of us must face on his or her own, when we have to bid the world good-night.

Underlying this poem is Gwenallt's powerful sense that there is no great distance between this world and the eternal world, no barriers which block our way towards God and God's way towards us, for his Kingdom has really drawn near to us. So, in one of his finest poems he sings of the nearness to us of the risen and ascended Christ, the one in whom the Kingdom is truly present. He sings of his nearness to us in all the simplicity of the sacraments of his love, made known to us in the coming of the life-giving Spirit, everywhere present and filling all things.

> He was imprisoned by his Jewish flesh and bones
> Within the confines of his country.
> But he gave them as living planks to the nailing
> To be raised from the grave, in spite of the guarding,
> As a catholic body by his Father.
>
> And now Cardiff is as near as Calvary
> Bangor every inch as near as Bethlehem.
> And storms in Cardigan Bay are stilled,
> And the afflicted on every street
> Find salvation at the touch of his hem.

He did not hide his gospel among the clouds of
  Judaea
Beyond the eye and tongue of man.
But he gives the life that lasts forever
In drop of wine and a crumb of bread
And the gift of the Spirit in the drops of water.[13]

Questions for discussion

1. Gwenallt was convinced that our faith should make its influence felt throughout our life – social, political and public as well as individual and domestic. His vision of Christianity was of a both/and kind, not of an either/or kind. Where do you stand on this question? Do you think it is possible to confine the influence of Christianity to our private lives?

2. For much of this century socialism seemed to many people to hold out the hope of a more just society. Was that hope altogether mistaken? What would we mean by Christian socialism today? What are the Christian foundations for the Welfare State? Should we be looking for a form of Christian capitalism?

3. In the earlier part of this century rich and poor people tended to live closer together in our cities. In our present society it is possible for the successful and affluent to get by without having any direct contact with the unsuccessful and deprived. What can we in particular do about this? Does your parish, for instance, get involved in such questions?

Chapter 5

Stages of Life's Journey
Guto'r Glyn

I
Introduction

We have looked at the life and work of two hymn-writers of the Methodist revival and at two major poets from our own century. We have seen in them the very varied ways in which it is possible to think of the Christian life as a journey, and to see the journey of each person as part of the pilgrimage of the whole of God's people. In the next two chapters, we come to the time before the Reformation, when the practice of pilgrimage was still a regular, public part of the Church's life, and we discover something of how people thought about the subject then.

In many ways the Middle Ages seem very far from us. But in this particular point they may come unexpectedly close. For, after four centuries of silence and neglect, in our own time the practice of pilgrimage has come to life again. In the course of our own century many of the ancient holy places of Britain have been renewed as places of prayer and gathering.

This happened first of all in the years after World War I, then more rapidly in the last half-century. So pilgrimages to holy places have become part of the experience of a great many people. Places like Iona in Scotland and

Resurrection's Children

Lindisfarne or Glastonbury in England have become known not only nationally but also internationally. The ancient Marian shrines of Walsingham in Norfolk and Haddington in Scotland have come to new life. The same thing is happening in Wales at Penrhys.

In Wales as a whole, however, this movement seems to have developed more slowly. But already by the 1950s Bishop J. C. Jones of Bangor was encouraging a renewal of pilgrimage to Bardsey Island (Ynys Enlli), one of the oldest pilgrimage places of Wales. In the last decade that pilgrimage has developed in a remarkable way. Another holy place which has come to new life, even more recently, has been the church of Pennant Melangell in its valley in the Berwyn Hills.[1]

One point of interest in all this is that it is not only pre-Reformation places of prayer which have attracted pilgrims in these years. In England, Little Gidding, the home of the Ferrar family in the seventeenth century, has become a place of pilgrimage, not least because of T. S. Eliot's poem about it. In Wales, the places associated with Ann Griffiths – Llanfihangel-yng-Gwynfa, Dolwar Fach, Dolanog and, perhaps above all, Hen Gapel John Hughes at Pontrobert – are attracting more visitors, some of them from far afield.

In these next two chapters we shall be looking at poems which bring us to two places, Pennant Melangell and Bardsey Island. Our general theme of journeying will take on a more explicit colour of pilgrimage. We shall be asking what it means to come to a place 'where prayer has been valid', and how it is that in such places the gulf between past and present often seems to be overcome.

Stages of Life's Journey

II
The building of a house

The fifteenth century is generally recognized as one of the richest periods in the whole long literary tradition of Wales. It produced a number of poets of outstanding quality, among them a man called Guto'r Glyn (*c*.1410–93). Guto is a writer who has not been considered particularly religious by modern commentators. He was a man of the world, a man of action, a man with a particular gift for friendship. Caerwyn Williams, the most distinguished of Welsh literary scholars, gives us a vivid picture of him:

> A big man with large knees and large hands, he appears to have had a broad face and a prominent nose, and a shock of black hair, some of which was prematurely lost, leaving a bald pate.... By nature warm-hearted, generous and loyal, he seems to have been able to evoke the same qualities in his patrons. Appreciative of fine fare, lively conversation and convivial company, not only was he humorous and witty himself, but he could also elicit humour and wit in his companions. Nature, it seems, had endowed him not only with the artistic gifts of a bard but also with a personality and disposition calculated to make him enjoy to the full the social life which was inextricably bound to the bardic profession.[2]

Amongst his contemporaries there are those like Lewis Glyn Cothi who deal more explicitly than he does with religious themes such as the praise of God, of Our Lady or of the saints. Because Guto'r Glyn's religion is so unself-consciously part of his whole attitude to life, he can tell us much about the fusion of faith and culture which characterized the later Middle Ages. This fusion had its limitations and weaknesses, which were to be exposed in the storms of the sixteenth-century Reformation. But it also had its strengths, some of them rooted in the earliest centuries of Celtic Christianity, which can be seen clearly in Guto'r Glyn's writing.

Guto'r Glyn was a man who, by medieval standards, lived an unusually long life. Some of his best-known poems today are those in which, as an old man, he celebrates the generous hospitality of the Abbot of Valle Crucis, in allowing him to stay in the monastery guest-house and be cared for there. These are poems in which, with a humour which is characteristic of him, Guto presents himself as a talkative, demanding old man, trying the patience of his hosts, yet deeply grateful for the refuge they offer him in his old age.

These poems of his latter years may be paralleled by others which suggest that he had a particularly strong sense of how human life has different stages with different gifts and different demands. As a young man he rejoices in the camaraderie of a military expedition into France in the last days of the Hundred Years War. He was evidently attracted by the soldier's life and was later strongly identified with the Yorkist cause in the Wars of the Roses in Wales.

He was not only a military man. He tried his hand at various occupations. We find, for instance, a poem of self-mockery which laments his lack of success as a sheep-dealer, driving his flock between English midland towns such as Coventry, Stafford and Lichfield. Then, in middle age, we find a poem which records the delights of life in a town, as he begins to appreciate urban living more fully and settles in Oswestry:

Stages of Life's Journey

Young, I was a hill-dweller;
now approaching man's age,
it's an old man's inclination
to lead his life in an urban place. . . .
He gets the warmth of urban life,
loves the white bread and the beer and the meat.
And the valley-land's wooden houses
will make me healthy, like a green tree.
Because of that, I have my dwelling
in the March, I'll have wine and mead.
It's a generous city to draw us,
the most gifted of cities,
the castle with the curtain wall,
and the best town till Rome.
Croesoswallt, friend of Jesus,
it was a great citadel for the conqueror.

London of the country of Owain and his land,
wine-filled houses and orchard-land,
it's a bright school of grace,
and a town of the preachers
and men of metre and grammar,
handling God in a beautiful temple.
The best church with an excellent chalice
and all its organ and its bells,
the best choir and artisans
and men and clothes till Canterbury.[3]

We get a clear picture of the attraction of life in a medieval town, of its comfort and its security. We see it centred on the church with its clergy, men of learning who daily offer up the body of Christ, 'handling God' in the sacrament of the altar. But we note too that Oswestry is called 'the London of Owain's land'. This is the district from which Owain Glyndwr came, and perhaps here and in other

Resurrection's Children

places we can see in the references to Glyndwr a sadness over a moment which has passed, a hope for a moment which may yet come.

Although we are not certain where Guto'r Glyn's birthplace was, it seems likely that he came from one of the valleys in the upland country to the west of Oswestry, possibly Dyffryn Ceiriog. Certainly, one of the closest of his patrons, Hywel ap Ieuan Fychan, builder of the house at Moelyrch, came from the neighbouring valley of Llansilin. In the case of Hywel we have a poem which describes the building of this new house. We are told that the house dominates its valley and can be seen from miles away. The same is true of the farm which today stands where the house was.

> A thousand see it on the hilltop
> Great its praise, how high it is. . . .

So prominent is its position that even at night-time, when it is lit up, it is still a landmark:

> It is no harder for us
> To go to it by night than by day;
> A hundred men of England see it,
> A candle and torch of Cynllaith it is.

This is a house built in a place which looks down to England. It is also less than two miles from Sycharth, Owain Glyndwr's residence, which had itself been praised in a similar poem in the previous century, but which had been totally destroyed by the English during the course of the Glyndwr rising. Guto'r Glyn nowhere says in this poem that he thinks of Moelyrch as a replacement for Sycharth, but it is difficult to think that the idea never came into his mind. This is particularly the case when he describes it as 'a hall like Owain's star', a reference to a comet which had appeared at the height of Glyndwr's rising. At the very least, the memory of Glyndwr must have been powerfully alive in that valley.

But all these local allusions are in the end eclipsed by the image with which the poem begins and ends. As often happens in Welsh and Irish poetry, the work is held together by a single image affirmed at its beginning and its conclusion. In the present poem the image is the temple of Jerusalem:

> From great trees David the prophet
> Made an edifice for the holy God....[4]

This work which David began was brought to conclusion by Solomon. So Hywel has brought to conclusion the design of his father, Ieuan Fychan. The Welsh nobleman's house is an image of the temple of God. It too has been a work which extended over two generations. So, at the end of his poem the writer invokes the patronage of Derfel, the saint of a nearby parish, and 'the patronage of Christ on his cruciform hall'. The house is an image of the temple of the old covenant; it is also an image of the cruciform hall, the Church of the new covenant.

Richard Loomis, commenting on Guto's work, points to the frequency with which he speaks of these gentry houses in terms of light. They are lights shining out like beacons into the darkness of the night, their glass windows (a new and expensive adjunct to the building) reflecting back the sun's rays. Speaking of Moelyrch in particular, the poet calls it the 'hillside's sun, *haul y fron*, shining like a mirror, with many doors....' The house stands high, facing south, catching the morning sun long before it reaches the village of Llansilin in the valley below. Its doors are opened wide to welcome Guto'r Glyn, revealing a warmth of hospitality within.

Guto'r Glyn is thus a poet who celebrates the building of new houses and the building up of the families who live in them, through the opening of their doors in hospitality to all who come. In one poem he writes:

> I have fashioned the song of a place like paradise,
> I fashion a song to advance the building.

The poet's work can augment the building itself and the life that it contains.

III

Confronting pain and loss

But human life is full of accidents. Hywel of Moelyrch wounded his knee in a fall from his horse. Knowing how delicate and complicated the mending of a knee can be, even with the help of late twentieth-century medical techniques, it is not difficult to imagine what it must have meant in the fifteenth century, when medical procedures were primitive and few. What is more, we remember that this was a time when, unless you rode a horse, you had to walk. In either case, a knee injury was an immense problem.

The healing *cywydd* which Guto'r Glyn writes to Hywel shows us something of the human reality of injury in this period. It also shows us something of the closeness of the relationship between poet and patron. Guto is deeply identified with Hywel in his misfortune. This is the theme which opens and concludes the poem.

However, before we begin to look at the poem in detail, it may be well to pause for a moment and consider the nature of this particular type of work. The purpose of all praise poems is, as we have seen, 'to recreate an unblemished world'. By lifting things up and offering them to God, from whom they came in the beginning, we see things in their original goodness, in the perspective of the God who sees all that he has made, and sees that it is good. So the poems of praise are meant to strengthen and affirm all that is good and beautiful in the person or animal or object that is praised.

Such poems may take different forms, in part according to the character of the subject praised; what is appropriate in one case will not be appropriate in another. But the form of praise may also vary according to the situation of the one who is being praised. In the case of injury or illness, the element of prayer or intercession in the poem will necessarily be strengthened. But the basic purpose of affirmation remains; only in this case it is centred on the thought of the restoration of health.

Guto begins, as we have said, with a powerful, direct affirmation of his sense of identity with the sufferer:

> Hywel ab Ieuan Fychan, I won't sleep much
> (a gray-white stag) because you're not well.
> My lot is anxiety
> if you're sick.
> If you're healed (God can do it)
> from your wound, I'm fine and very fit.
> If you're sick, my Mordaf,
> sick, weak do I feel myself too.
> Your sad fall takes me out of my good state,
> your joint brings me affliction.

He goes on to say how all the people of the district – Hywel's tenants and retainers, no less than his neighbours and friends – were affected by this wound. He, a fully qualified bard, Hywel's own poet, mourned; but so too,

Resurrection's Children

at least for a time, did the wandering minstrels, the lesser entertainers whom the great poets tended to regard as beneath their notice:

> All the world was threatened (yours is a beautiful
>   nature)
> because of your knee-pan.
> I wept in Moelyrch,
> the size of the fall, a troop seek him out.
> The wandering poets were sad for your great wound;
> I'm still sad for you.

There follow four lines in which Guto thinks of all the people whom he would have liked to see in trouble, and they bring us to the only two lines in the poem where the poet speaks directly of medical assistance, in the reference to Hippocrates:

> A pity is the bandage on a generous man;
> we mourn that a stingy man didn't get it.
> By the true God, I'd laugh
> if it were on some of those I know!
> Hippocrates (a noble David)
> will pull you free of the bandage.

Much more space is given to Hywel's wife, who is seen as fulfilling the role of Mary Magdalen in relation to Jesus. Unfortunately, the poet has not noticed that the woman at Bethany anointed Jesus for his burial and not for healing! These lines are followed by four lines celebrating the warmth of summer – lines which surely refer to the warmth of human care and affection which 'the beautiful Elen brings':

> A Mary Magdalen is modest Elen,
> she cares for you, a long task.
> The salve of the woman who was Jesus' physician

made a dear remedy,
and with her salve
may beautiful Elen's efforts do the same for your knee.
One who'd love eaves and the fresh woods
and God's grace and the day's warmth
and the virtue of summer's nature
will break the pangs of winter.

Guto then comes to himself, and calls to his assistance Taliesin, his kinsman. The historical Taliesin had lived some nine centuries before Guto's time, but for Guto he is still a kinsman, closely related in the synchronicity of the poetic tradition, in which the past has not passed away but is still experienced as present. In this paragraph we have the most powerful image to be found in the whole poem, where the poet speaks of 'the prison of the wound'. The restriction of mobility to an able, active man, needing to get about his estates, to visit his neighbours, possibly to undertake a military expedition at the behest of his king or his feudal lord, is felt bitterly.

Here too we have Guto's explicit assertion of the healing power of poetry as of something well known: 'many a person was healed with a *cywydd*'. But at the end of this paragraph, when he has promised to make an ointment of praise, he suddenly acknowledges his own limitation. If this doesn't work, then we must turn to the powers of heaven:

The sound of the poetry of our kinsman Taliesin
got his master out of prison.
I have a mind, because of what I might compose,
to get the knee out of the prison of the wound.
Many a person (you're golden-handed)
was healed with a cywydd.

Resurrection's Children

> I swear by the fire, I too
> will make an ointment of praise for you.
> And if the mouth (and what it made)
> doesn't have the power of a medication,
> the host of heaven will make you merrily well.

At this point, before we come to the last section of the poem, it may be good to look back at a statement about Hywel's healing made at the beginning – the parenthetic remark, 'God can do it.' The whole poem is placed under that rubric. It is not, as at times it seems to be, an exercise in sympathetic magic. It is the gathering together of many kinds of human endeavour, all invoked with the proviso that in the end it is God who must decide.

But now, before we come to the final appeal to heaven's Lord, we appeal to the company of heaven and in particular to a number of saints, many of whom are near neighbours. There is Silin, the patron of the parish church; Oswald, the martyr-saint who protected Oswestry; Gwenfrewi, another martyr-saint whose holy waters at Holywell, not so far away, were specially noted for their qualities of healing. Then, having called upon Christ himself (here we observe a lack of proportion which was perhaps typical of the lay piety of the age, in that the King of the saints is simply included in the list), we come to the final climax of the poem, 'go to Melangell'. The essential thing will be to make a pilgrimage over the ten miles or so to the church of Pennant Melangell, another woman saint whose shrine was known both as a place of sanctuary and as a place of healing.

> Behold! everybody's merrier!
> Generous Saint Silin (better than the chill of an
>   ointment)
> blesses you;

Stages of Life's Journey

> Oswald, the fine-haired king,
> will rid the knee of the leg-wound;
> Mary, with your gold and myrrh and incense;
> may Martin be assisting!
> Gwenfrewi will fully overcome complaint and disease,
> injury and wound.
> The miracles of Ieuan of Gwanas
> will drive it from the knee, with the silver cross.
> Curig will be your physician;
> Christ himself, of execution's Cross.
> With Saint Lednart, our kinsman, we'll get
> to fetch you out of prison.
> Go to Melangell now,
> arise, O Nudd, you'll get to be well.

Then abruptly the poem ends as it began, with the poet's identification with his friend. After all the calling on the powers of heaven, there is a simple, bare expression of human identification with human suffering and distress:

> I won't sing bold praise poetry,
> I won't laugh until you walk.[5]

IV

Friendships of strength and beauty

This poem is a remarkable example of a work which is not only a simple but powerful human wish – a highly developed 'Get well' card – but also an act of prayer, confiding everything to God. As a healing exercise it is remarkable in that it follows one of the basic principles of holistic medicine, seeking to involve all those who are related to the sufferer, whether his tenants, his neighbours, his wife or his closest friends.

It is also, as one examines and re-examines it, an expression of real compassion and deep and practical love. The medieval Welsh poets sometimes spoke of themselves as carpenters of song. Guto, in one place, speaks of himself as a carpenter of love. Loomis comments:

> in calling himself a carpenter of love, Guto may mean simply that he is a carpenter-like craftsman inspired by love. Or, he may mean that he is a carpenter of love itself, one who can shape friendships of strength and beauty, that resemble wood-carvings as achievements of human art, a shaping of the raw stuff of nature into harmonious and dynamic civility.

With his praise Guto 'recreates an unblemished world'.

The poem, although clearly anchored in the fifteenth century, show signs of carrying in itself traces of much older poetic conventions. We have said that it is not a work of sympathetic magic, and yet, in its reference to Taliesin, it clearly conveys suggestions of some long pre-Christian confidence in the healing power of the poetic word itself. The fire that is spoken of in these lines is, we may reasonably suppose, a reference to the fire of a divine inspiration, which will concoct the healing remedy for the wound.

But the poem not only reflects a very ancient understanding of the therapeutic power of the poetic word; it also reflects a very ancient and long pre-Christian view of the relationship between the poet and his patron. In early Irish poetry, and still in the poetry of the seventeenth century in Ireland, there is a powerful convention in which the poet speaks of himself as his patron's wife. It is the same here in fifteenth-century Wales. Guto has a whole poem addressed to Hywel in which he speaks of them bound together with bonds stronger than those which link husband and wife in marriage. Andrew Breeze comments:

> Pledging solemn loyalty to Hywel ap Ieuan Fychan of Moelyrch ... he speaks of his union to Hywel as a marriage.... His union with Hywel is no harum scarum Gretna Green affair, but a grave, solemn, advised, deliberate, holy and permanent matter entered into after long consideration.... Guto's testimonies to the bonding of poet and patron show a continuity going back to the days of Celtic paganism.[6]

It is difficult to know how to read and interpret such a poem, which reflects social conventions and attitudes so different from our own. Guto himself seems to recognize that in claiming this particular relationship with Hywel he is making a claim which will be strongly contested. There are others, he says, who are angry that they do not receive precisely this kind of praise. Guto had many patrons in different parts of Wales, whose hospitality and generosity he praised and celebrated in a great variety of ways; but somehow these relationships were not the same. He refers specifically to the bonds of deep friendship which link him to Dafydd ap Ieuan, Abbot of Valle Crucis; but he says the marriage bond which he claims with Hywel is not something appropriate in the case of someone in holy orders.

What is particularly striking is a passage in the middle of the poem where Guto speaks of the bond between himself and Hywel in the same breath as he speaks of his gift and activity as a poet. It would be difficult, he says, twice, for him as a poet not to give expression to this love. These lines not only express an ancient and, to us, puzzling convention, but also seem to be written under the strong pressure of human emotion.[7]

Reading such a passage, I have been reminded of words spoken by a great Orthodox theologian, Father Dumitru Staniloae: 'There are, I think, as many kinds of love and friendship as there are human persons.' It seems that we have too narrow and stereotyped a view of the nature of personal love, something which can be infinitely various and inventive.

In reading the history of long-past times, it is important to recognize that 'The past is another country.' It is vital to recognize the strangeness of the evidence, which often will not fit into our way of seeing things, but which can sometimes alter our understanding of things and show us patterns of life and meaning which we have not seen before, as long as we are attentive to what is there and let the facts speak to us. In a similar way, when reading the books of the Bible, it is important to let the texts from the past speak to us in their own terms, without our trying to impose our wishes and desires on them.

However, one thing is common to the fifteenth century and today. The theme of the journey through life, and especially the journey through sickness and healing, or lack of healing, towards death, is one which carries with it the thought of the necessity of companionship. It is a theme particularly appropriate for this most sociable pet. We need to be able to travel together, to journey in company. In Guto'r Glyn's poems we see many different aspects of this travelling together, some of which are Christian, some of which are pre-Christian. We find ourselves in a world in which faith and culture are spontaneously fused into one, a world which can confidently call upon God and his saints, at moments when the traveller seems altogether shut in, confined in the prison of the wound.

Stages of Life's Journey

Questions for discussion

1. As an old man Guto'r Glyn was cared for in the Abbey of Valle Crucis and remained active as a poet even when he had lost his sight. Does this pattern of life have something to say to us today? How far do we encourage old people to be themselves and to rejoice in the presence of God?

2. Medieval people had very few medical resources compared with ourselves. Did they make up for their lack of medical knowledge by their faith and prayer and care for others? How far do we combine intercession, medical care and ordinary human concern in our approach to the sick?

3. Perhaps in the Middle Ages people thought too much about the approach of death. Do we think about it at all? How far is preparation for death a necessary part of Christian living? Is it possible to live fully without some thought of the end to which our life is moving? How do you approach this question?

Chapter 6

The Isle of Expectation
Meilyr Brydydd

I
Introduction

We come at the end of this book to the earliest of the writers we shall consider, to a poem which deals directly with our theme of the journey through death to life, our pilgrimage through time to eternity.

In this poem, which was written in about 1140, the poet faces the prospect of death and prays for God's forgiveness for the sins of his life. It is a deathbed poem, a *marwysgafn*, a type of poem fully recognized in medieval Welsh. It has a very special quality because it is also a poem in which the poet prays that his final pilgrimage may be one that is made to the island of Enlli (Bardsey). Like thousands of others in pre-Reformation Wales, he prays that he may die on that holy island, in the fellowship of its community, confident that Enlli is not only his place of death but also his place of resurrection.

It is a rightly famous poem, the work of a rightly famous poet. Meilyr Brydydd is one of the earliest, if not indeed the earliest, of the Poets of the Princes. These were a group of writers who have a special place in the Welsh tradition. In the period from 1120 to 1280, they carried their poetic art to a high point of power and sophistication, using all

The Isle of Expectation

their rhetorical skills to strengthen the Welsh princes in the last century and a half of their struggle for independence. The poem is also well known because it is one of a small group of texts which suddenly, at the beginning of this period, reveal to us something of the reason for the long-standing renown of Enlli as a place of pilgrimage.

There are many mysteries which surround that island. We have little, if any, written evidence for its life and character before the eleventh century. In the case of Iona in Scotland or Lindisfarne in northern England – both holy islands which attracted, and still attract, great numbers of pilgrims – we have a great deal of early written evidence to tell us about their history. We can read the story of Columba and his companions on Iona as told by Adomnan; we can read the life of Aidan and Cuthbert, as recounted by Bede, and we can see their connections with Lindisfarne. But with Enlli, for whatever reason, there is nothing, before 1100 except what we learn indirectly from the reputation which the island had already gained by that time as a place of great antiquity and a place of great holiness, the burial-place of a multitude of saints.

Then suddenly there comes a series of witnesses to the fame of the island as a place of outstanding holiness, the island of the twenty thousand saints, which can be compared with Rome itself as a place where God's presence is to be found. Let us look at two of these texts. In 1120, at the moment when the newly built cathedral in Llandaff in South Wales was being consecrated, the relics of St Dyfrig were solemnly transferred from Enlli to the new cathedral. The fact that it was believed that Dyfrig was buried on Enlli is itself quite extraordinary. Not only is Dyfrig one of the earliest saints of Wales – a man who flourished in the latter part of the fifth century – but also he is a saint whose centre of operations was in the extreme south-east

Resurrection's Children

of Wales, often in what is now called Herefordshire, as far from Enlli as can be. Yet, so it was said, he had retired to Enlli at the end of his life. The translation of the relics in 1120 was for Dyfrig a kind of return to his home country.

Dyfrig, more than anyone else, stands for the continuities between the churches in Roman Britain and the churches which, in the fifth century, were regrouping themselves in the west as more and more of the eastern parts of Britain fell into the hands of the Anglo-Saxon invaders. Thus he is a link with the churches in the time of the Roman occupation. The very fact that it could be thought that he had come to Enlli at the end of his life and had been buried there already tells us much about the significance of the island to the Christians of the earliest centuries in Wales.

In a document written at the time of the consecration of Llandaff Cathedral, we read one of the earliest descriptions of the island:

> It has been for ages a proverbial saying among the Welsh that this island is the 'Rome of Britain', on account of its distance – it is situated in the extremity of the kingdom – and the danger of the sea voyage, and also because of the holiness and charm of the place; holiness, for twenty thousand bodies of the saints, both confessors and martyrs, lie buried there; charm, since it is surrounded by the sea with a lofty headland on the eastern side and a level, fertile plain where there is a spring of sweet water, on the western side.[1]

To anyone who knows the island, this description at once rings true; it seems to turn its back on the mainland and to look out over the sea to Ireland and the Wicklow Hills.

Sixty years later, in 1188, Gerald of Wales, on his tour through Wales with Baldwin, Archbishop of Canterbury, heard more about the character of the place:

The Isle of Expectation

> Beyond Llŷn there is a small island occupied by some extremely devout monks called *coelibes* or *colidei*. Either because of its pure air which comes across the sea from Ireland, or because of some miracle occasioned by the merits of the holy men who live there the island has this peculiarity, that no-one dies there except of extreme old age, for disease is almost unheard of. In fact no-one dies there at all unless he is very old indeed. The bodies of a vast number of holy men are buried there, or so they say, among them that of Deiniol, Bishop of Bangor.[2]

It is striking that this story of a monastery in which only the oldest die, and where, when they do so, they die in strict order of seniority, is also told of Landevennec, the great monastic centre of western Brittany. There too they found it difficult to die. From the beginning there were connections between Enlli and Brittany. Cadfan, the first abbot of the island, is reputed to have come from Brittany with his companions. But there were also links with Ireland, as Gerald's account makes clear. The monks on Bardsey had been influenced by the *culdee* movement, the ninth-century Irish movement of monastic renewal and reform. Being an island in a world of sea communications, Bardsey was a place of many contacts. Indeed, the island could be seen as a kind of hinge or meeting-point between the two parts of the old Celtic world: the countries of Brythonic speech on the one side – Wales, Cornwall and Brittany – and the countries of Gaelic speech on the other – Ireland, Man and Western Scotland.

Here, then, we have an island off the north-west tip of Wales, a place of pilgrimage for people from the south and east no less than from the north and west, an island which was very easily visited by anyone travelling from North Wales to Dublin. It is to this island that Meilyr longs to come.

II
The partnership of prince and poet

But before we come to look at the poem we must think a little more about the poet himself and the Prince of Gwynedd whom he served, Gruffudd ap Cynan. Meilyr Brydydd was a poet who flourished in the first half of the twelfth century. Not only was he the first of the poets of the princes, reputedly the founder of a new school of poetry, but he was also the father of a family of poets. His son Gwalchmai followed in his footsteps, and Gwalchmai was then succeeded by three sons of his own, Einion ap Gwalchmai, Meilyr ap Gwalchmai and Elidir Sais. They were a family of some substance on Anglesey. Two closely connected place-names on the island today – Trefeilyr and Trewalchmai – still speak of the impression they made there.[3]

That the poet's gift should descend from one generation to another in the same family was not something unfamiliar in the early Christian centuries in Wales and Ireland, though it is much more often recorded in Ireland than in Wales. As well as being a gift to be received, poetry was also an exacting craft to be learnt through years of disciplined study, so what could be more proper than that it should be handed on directly from father to son?

It is probably not by chance that we find this Irish characteristic in the family of Meilyr, for he and the prince whom he served had very close connections with Ireland. Gruffudd ap Cynan is a vital but enigmatic figure in the history of medieval Wales. Born near the middle of the eleventh century, he died at a great age in 1137. Much of his boyhood was spent in exile in Ireland. While on his father's side he was descended from the kings of North Wales, through his

The Isle of Expectation

mother he was descended from king Brian Boru of Ireland and king Harold Fairhair of Norway. Gruffudd was evidently very proud of this international lineage.

The first fifty years of his life were full of turmoil, fighting and instability as he tried, in the face of various rivals, to establish himself as prince in North Wales. Twice at least he had to flee back to Ireland. For ten years or more he was held as a prisoner by the Normans in Chester. Only towards the end of his life did he finally assert his position as ruler over the kingdom of Gwynedd.

It seems that in the end he established himself very firmly there. When he died he left behind the reputation of a king who had made a space for peace and order in a notably violent and unstable world. He was certainly a great benefactor of the Church, and it is interesting to note that he was present in the south at the consecration of Llandaff Cathedral in 1120, when St Dyfrig's relics were translated there from Bardsey. As a ruler of Gwynedd, he would have been closely involved in such an event.

In words which are certainly idealized but nonetheless significant, his biographer tells us of this last period of his life:

> then every kind of good increased in Gwynedd and the people began to build churches in every place therein, to sow woods and plant them, to cultivate orchards and gardens, and surround them with fences and ditches, to construct walled buildings and live on the fruits of the earth after the fashion of the men of Rome. Gruffudd also built large churches in his own major court and held his courts and feasts always honourably. Furthermore Gwynedd glittered then with lime-washed churches like the firmament with stars.[4]

Resurrection's Children

A nomadic way of life was giving way to a more settled one, and the first stone-built churches were replacing their fragile wooden predecessors.

In all this work of building and education the poet Meilyr would have been involved. The bonds which linked the court poet with his prince were very close indeed. He was, as it were, Gruffudd's minister of information, chief spokesman and official historian. Apart from the deathbed poem, which we shall examine later, the only surviving poem of Meilyr which we have is his elegy for Gruffudd. In it he gives us glimpses of his own position of influence in the court:

> I drink with the king from golden drinking horns. . . .
> I for my part took my choice
> from among the war-horses in the yard of his court. . . .

Perhaps above all his pride in his position is revealed in the lines

> At the court at Aberffraw
> Beside the ruler I was enthroned.

But his relationship with the prince was not only an outward and political matter. We are made to pause when suddenly the poet tells us that their relationship has a totally different dimension to it. It is rooted in a relationship made in God:

> I shall not break my friendship with my friend,
> The friendship which is according to the Trinity.

All true, faithful, loving relationships within the human family have their foundation in the eternal relationships which exist between the persons of the Trinity. The poet reveals himself to be a powerful expositor of the deepest core of Christian faith.

Professor Caerwyn Williams remarks that the word for

The Isle of Expectation

'friendship' here, *cerennydd*, has 'rich connotations. Its usual meanings are kindred, kinship, relationship, descent, affinity; friendship, love, reconciliation.'[5] It touches both the world of family relationships and that of personal friendship. This is a relationship which we come to know according to the Trinity, when human life is lived in the image and likeness of the triune God. This is the eternal reality which underlies the passion and the violence, the pride and the longing which we see in this remote and early medieval society; a society in which the king reigns and the poet affirms his reign.

III

Preparing the last journey

So, as he approaches his death, Meilyr comes before God with the whole rich, mixed experience of life which has been his and addresses his creator as Rex Regum, King of Kings:

> Rex regum, for whom praise flows freely,
> To my Lord above I offer prayer:
> Prince of glory's land, pure region on high,
> Master, make peace between you and me.
> Sickened, saddened in heart that I have
> Offended you, remorseful for it,
> I have rated rebuke in God's presence,
> My true belief left unpractised:
> I will practise it yet, for my Prince,
> Before I am buried, left strengthless.
> True the prediction to Adam's offspring
> That has been proclaimed by the prophets:
> Jesus within Mary's virgin womb,
> Mary joyfully bore her burden.

> A burden have I built of sins heaped high;
> I have lived in fear of its turmoil.
> Lord of all places, how good to praise you!
> May I praise you, be purged before I burn.
> King of kings who knows me, deny me not
> Forgiveness for my transgressions.

The poem is addressed to Christ, as its opening words make clear. The title 'King of Kings, Lord of Lords' is used of Christ twice in the Book of Revelation (17:14; 19:16). It is the verse in chapter 17 which perhaps comes closest to the intention of this poem, for there the title is used specifically for the Lamb who conquers through his death. Meilyr's poem is addressed to Christ, who is both King and Judge. But the one who is King and Judge is also Creator and Redeemer. The titles which assert power and authority are joined with those which speak of gentleness and compassion.

So, although this is a deathbed poem which looks forward to the final judgement, its basic mood is not primarily one of fear, guilt and anxiety about sin – though all those things are present – but one of confidence and hope in a God whose final word is not condemnation but mercy, not death but resurrection.

It is interesting to notice that in some of the manuscripts of later Anglo-Saxon England these same titles, *Rex Regum* and *Dominus Dominantium*, are to be found written on the garments of Christ who comes as Judge. However, Paul Bryant-Quinn makes this observation:

> in two late Anglo-Saxon manuscripts these apocalyptic titles are directly associated with the image of the crucified ... [with] a striking image of Christ standing stripped and with arms outstretched, as at the crucifixion. To the discerning eye however, the hidden divinity of the crucified

The Isle of Expectation

is revealed not only in Christ's hieratic stance, but in the letters inscribed in his hair and halo which ingeniously spell out his true identity: *Iste Rex iustitiae* and *Rex Regum et Dominus Dominantium*.[6]

The religious and theological intuitions of late Anglo-Saxon England and those of twelfth-century Wales a century later come very close to one another. In both there is a complex fusion of mercy and judgement, of death and resurrection. So, in the very first line of this poem, Christ is addressed with confidence as one for whom praise flows freely, and in the second stanza the poet reiterates 'Lord of all places, how good it is to praise you!' Thus the Christ who comes as Judge is also the Christ who is Creator, the Christ who knows and cares about his creation. The initiative in the work of reconciliation is his, as is made very clear in the prayer in the fourth line: 'Master, make peace between you and me.' However different the style and approach may be from that of the eighteenth-century hymn-writers whose work we have looked at, here they are at one. God takes the initiative in the work of our redemption. Reconciliation and atonement begin in the holiness and love of God.

There are a number of places where the reading of the poem is difficult and disputed, in particular in line thirteen, with its reference to the womb of Mary. In the original there is a reference here to the martyrs, which this translation has simply omitted. There are technical questions here about possible corruptions of the text and the metre of the line in the original, which we need not go into. The interpretation which seems to me most satisfying is one which sees Jesus within the womb of Mary, who is the Queen of the Martyrs.[7] The suggestion, then, is that the joy of the birth of the Christ-child carries within it the future agony of

Resurrection's Children

the cross. The child who is born is the child who is to die. Mary herself is intimately associated with this suffering; already, in chapter 2 of St Luke's Gospel, she hears the words, 'a sword shall pierce your own soul also'. Again we see the idea that Christ who is the Judge is also Christ the Redeemer, a thought we shall find most fully developed in the climax in the final section of the poem.

In the second half of the poem the poet speaks out directly in his own person. He looks back over his work in praise of earthly princes and sees both its achievements and its failings; he laments that he has not given himself more to the praise of the King of Heaven. Now, his tongue falls silent. As his poem grows in strength and meaning, so he assures us that he can no longer sing. We are reminded of R. S. Thomas' words at the beginning of one of his most beautiful short poems, celebrating the church at Llananno: 'There are no poems in it for me.' Here, as there, the disclaimer is disproved by the movement of the verse itself.

> I have often had gold and brocade
> From mortal lords for singing their praise,
> And the gift of song gone, powers failing,
> Stripped of wealth my tongue fell silent.
> I, Meilyr the poet, pilgrim to Peter,
> Gate-keeper who gauges true value,
> At the time set for us to arise
> Who are in the grave, make me ready.
> May I dwell while awaiting the summons
> In the cell with the tide beside it:
> Secluded it is, undimmed its fame,
> With its graves in the breast of the sea,
> Fair Mary's isle, saintly isle of her saints,
> Resurrection's scene, it is splendid.
> Christ, his cross foretold, will know me, lead me

The Isle of Expectation

Past the pains of hell, exile's dwelling.
The Maker who made me will meet me
In the fair parish of Enlli's faithful.[8]

As often happens in this early poetry of praise, the poet presents himself directly to us. Here, however, he declares himself not only in his personal calling but also in the role which his society has always acknowledged in him – 'I, Meilyr the poet', now pilgrim to Peter – and he goes on to pray that he may await the day of final judgement 'In a cell with the tide beside it:/Secluded it is, undimmed its fame'.

The word which is here translated 'secluded' is *didryf* in the original. It is a word which means 'desert, wilderness, solitary or uninhabited land'. In his dictionary of 1632 Dr John Davies points out that from this word comes the meaning *Religio monastica vel eremitica*, 'the monastic or solitary way of life'. It is one of the technical terms in medieval Welsh for the hermit vocation. Bardsey had always been a place for such a life as well as for community life, and its most famous eleventh-century representative was the hermit Elgar, who was also involved in the Llandaff consecration of 1120.

The island, a place of solitude, lies in the breast of the sea. Its graveyard, (*mynwent*) lies in the embrace (*mynwes*) of the salt sea. This is Mary's Isle, and just as the King of the martyrs waited in her womb to be born, so here we await our allotted time in the island's place of burial and find that it is for us a place of new birth and new creation. 'Fair Mary's isle, pure isle of the pure/Resurrection's scene, to be in it is splendid.'

Here again the full meaning of the line becomes clear when we turn to the text of the original. The island is called *gwrthrych dadwyrain*. In modern Welsh the word *gwrthrych* means 'object', and it can also mean 'objective, aim, purpose, hope, expectation'. Here the word has a technical meaning related to the last sense. It is a term found in both Irish and Welsh medieval law, meaning 'the one who inherits, the heir apparent, the prince's successor'. The island itself is the heir of resurrection. It is in active expectation of new creation. As St Paul tells us, the whole creation waits in eager expectation for the manifestation of the sons of God.

I shall never forget the eager enthusiasm with which Sir Idris Foster expounded the meaning of this word to me some thirty or more years ago. I had asked him why this word, which I had understood to mean 'object', was used in this place. I had asked more than I knew. I felt as if I had put a match into a haystack. His exposition overflowed with an erudition which, at that time, I could hardly begin to take in. He ranged from the rules about succession in medieval Irish courts to the understanding of the resurrection in the Fathers of the Church. I was made vividly aware that, almost by chance, I had come across a powerful image, pregnant with meaning, in a remarkably powerful poem.

We come to the last four lines of the poem. The Christological theme announced at the very beginning is taken up again. Christ, whose cross is foretold from all eternity, Christ whose death is the destruction of death, is the one who has created me and who knows me. It is he who will deliver me from evil, lead me past the pains of hell – the place of exile and separation – and meet me 'in the fair parish of Enlli's faithful'. Like the farmer of Ty Pellaf some seven and a half centuries later, Meilyr puts all his confidence in Christ's life-giving cross.[9]

It might seem at first that there is almost an element of anticlimax here. Should not the poem open out at the end on to a heavenly perspective, to the host of heaven gathered around the Lord? Such poems often do. No, we stay where we are, with Enlli; it is here that the Lord will meet me and all who are his in this place. And with a great economy of words the poet goes on to tell us something of the true nature of the Christian community, a reality more many-sided and many-levelled than we often realize.

The word which he uses to speak of the community on the island – an island which, as we have seen, is as monastic as an island can be – is *plwyf*, the ordinary Welsh word for 'parish', which comes from the Latin word *plebs*, meaning 'the common people of God'. Parish and monastery are not separate or opposed to one another. There is a coinherence and interpenetration of calling within the family of the Church. The monastic family here, in medieval Welsh, is spoken of as a parish, just as in modern Irish the word for 'monastery', *muintir*, has come to be the word which speaks of the common people, the people of the land. We see something of the integral relationship between the monastic and lay communities which was one of the most striking features of the early centuries of the Church in the lands of Celtic speech and culture.

IV

Light in a dark world

The world in which the people of the early Middle Ages lived was in many ways a very simple one. If you wanted to travel from one place to another you had to use your legs, unless you had the resources which made it possible to travel on horseback. If you wanted a light at night-time, if you were lucky, there were candles and rush lights – nothing more. Land travel was so slow and dangerous that people often preferred to travel by sea, despite the hazards

Resurrection's Children

involved in sea journeys in small and fragile boats. So, as an island, Enlli was accessible, but paradoxically, it was also inaccessible, since none of the landing-places were particularly safe and easy before the nineteenth century.

Sea communication was of vital importance. Gwynedd was still, in the twelfth century, part of the old Celtic sea-world, with links to Cornwall and Brittany in the south and to the Orkneys and Norway in the north, and with a constant interchange with Ireland in the west. One of the most decisive battles of Gruffudd's reign occurred in 1098 when a large Viking fleet appeared unexpectedly off the coast of Anglesey and helped to defeat the Norman forces under Hugh of Shrewsbury.

We should not idealize this period of history or imagine that all was beautiful in it. The lives of kings, princes and chieftains were largely preoccupied with fighting – between peoples of the same language and between peoples of different languages. The Welsh system of dividing up the inheritance of a prince or chieftain between his sons led to endless family feuds, murders and mutilations. In 1125, for instance, Gruffudd's eldest son killed his three maternal uncles, Gruffudd's brothers-in-law.[10] Was this done at his father's instigation or despite his resistance? We do not know. Whichever way it was, it is an incident which helps us to understand more of the background of Meilyr Brydydd's two surviving poems, his elegy for the prince and his deathbed poem of repentance. It gives us a sense of the world out of which the latter poem came – its violence, brutality and unpredictability. It also gives us a new sense of the quality of miracle which informs the poem.

Out of such a world, so full of darkness, such a poem can be made. We are reminded of Andrei Tarkovsky's film about the life and work of the icon painter Andrei Rublev. The film is remarkable in many ways, not least in that it was made during the period of Soviet rule. After showing us at length, in black and white, the brutalities and violence of fourteenth-century Russia, in its last ten minutes the film moves into colour, and quietly shows us the serenity and peace which shine out of Rublev's frescoes. In the medieval Celtic world too works of great and healing beauty could be made.

Such violence and brutality are not things confined to the past. The twentieth century, which is now nearing its end, is one which has been filled with fearful acts of destruction and cruelty. We can at times feel altogether overwhelmed by the darkness of our world. The companionship of past ages – a new sense of the communion of saints across space and time – can help to give us courage and hope and can make it more possible for us to face the things which most daunt and paralyse us.

Here in our poem we have a man facing his own death, facing it with that sense of personal anguish, fear and guilt which is common enough to human beings as they reach that point of no return. Yet, despite its formality of style, it is a deeply personal poem, and this is doubtless the reason for its popularity in recent years. There are no less than seven translations into English. And despite its sense of anxiety and fear, its deepest note is one of praise: 'Lord of all places, how good it is to praise you.'

If Meilyr's poem is a personal statement, it is in no sense a private one. The poet comes before his Maker and Redeemer in solidarity with and as a representative of the society to which he belongs. The smallness of that society means that he holds together in himself different worlds which, with us, are usually widely separated: the world of politics and diplomacy; the world of fighting and violent

Resurrection's Children

action; the world of poetry and inherited learning; the world of prayer and sacramental worship; and, at least to some extent, the world of a monastic community and the world of a monastic solitary. All these things are combined together in this one life.

It is this fact which gives this poem such a remarkable sense of human richness. It holds together a many-levelled experience of life, with its horror and its beauty, its failure and its success, its grief and its joy, its times of activity and its time of contemplation. It holds all this together in a particular place, a place which is not marginal but central to this world, a place which the poet has chosen to be his place of death and burial, because he sees it as the place of his resurrection.

Meilyr's outlook on life is rooted in his Christian faith and his vision of an eternal purpose for himself and for all creation. *Cerennydd*, true friendship, is according to the Trinity. Human beings, as social beings, are made in the image and likeness of a God who is, within himself, the fullness of social being and the overflowing source of friendship. As Gerard Casey remarks, 'Only a pluralistic [i.e. Trinitarian] theism can give true, eternal significance to freedom realising itself in personal relationships, that is in friendship. Christ said to his disciples "I call you friends."'[11]

Thus, for the poet, even the encounter with death is an encounter with the Creator who knows and guides him, the Creator who has revealed the fullness of his love in the cross which was foretold. This is the design of great love foretold from all eternity. As Rublev has shown us in his icon of the Holy Trinity, and as the hymn-writers of the eighteenth century constantly affirm, in the cross we see that sacrificial love is at the heart of the Godhead. The King of Kings and Lord of Lords to whom the poem is addressed is the triumphant Lamb, the Lamb slain from

The Isle of Expectation

the foundation of the world (Revelation 5:6, 13:8). This is indeed a poem which unfolds to us the mystery of Easter in all its height and depth, in all its length and breadth.

Questions for discussion

1. It has been said that 'The past is a foreign country.' When we study a book of the Bible or the life of a saint who lived many centuries ago, do we make allowance for all the differences which the passage of time makes, and do we bear in mind the ways in which our culture differs from that of the people who wrote the book? On the other hand, do we remember the things which link us with the past across the centuries, especially our faith in God and our experience of his love?

2. In a century of much turmoil, Meilyr Brydydd glimpsed something of the peace and serenity of God's Kingdom. Do we allow ourselves to be overwhelmed by the genocides and disasters of our own time, or do we find how to deepen our faith in the triumph of good over evil, of light over darkness, through the victory of Christ's cross?

3. We have seen in many places in this book that 'friendship according to the Trinity' is vital for human life. Have we grown in friendship through our lives? Have we perhaps grown in friendship through studying this book?

Conclusion

The End which is a Beginning

The great affirmation of Easter night, as it is made above all in the Eastern Orthodox Churches, is an affirmation of incomparable power. Good has triumphed over evil, love has triumphed over hatred, life has triumphed over death. The constantly repeated verse, 'Christ is risen from the dead, trampling down death by death and to those in the tombs giving life', sets the tone for the whole celebration. It is an affirmation at once particular and specific, springing from the cross and the empty tomb outside Jerusalem, yet at the same time universal in its scope. In Christ's rising all in the tombs are set free; and surely that includes those of us who are still alive as well as those who have already died, for we are all in one kind of tomb or another.

The insistent words of the celebrant's greeting, 'Christ is risen', and the immediate response of the congregation, 'He is risen indeed', gather us in to the action. The words of the canon of St John of Damascus, with their joy in the resurrection, are at once personal and universal. The words of the sermon of St John Chrysostom about the workers who come at the eleventh hour and who are welcomed in the same way as those who came at the first hour, underline the all-embracing character of the event which we are celebrating. Easter is for all. Christ is risen, and there are no more dead in the tombs.

On one occasion many years ago, as I was leaving the Church of the St Sergius Institute in Paris at the end of the

The End which is a Beginning

Easter vigil, I had the thought, 'Even if God didn't exist, there could be no greater affirmation of human life and existence than this!'

But of course, our Western liturgy for the night of Easter, in its new and restored form, is no less striking. Indeed, in many ways it is even richer in symbolism and meaning. There is the lighting of the new fire at the outset, and the lighting of the paschal candle which follows: 'The light of Christ which rises gloriously cast out all darkness from each heart and mind.' Then comes the tremendous affirmation of the *Exultet*, in which the light of Easter night is seen to shed its light back over the whole of human history, so that even the sin of Adam can be seen as somehow necessary, foreseen in view of the greater good of redemption and resurrection to come.

There follows the long series of readings from the Old Testament, starting with Genesis and going on to Exodus and the visions of the prophets – readings which emphasize the closeness of creation to resurrection. Here is the fulfilment of God's purpose from the beginning. Then there may be the Baptism and Confirmation of those being initiated into the Church, and certainly for all there is the renewal of baptismal vows, leading us into the Eucharist of Easter, which brings us into a new covenant relationship with God and with all things. Here again the struggle between light and darkness, between hope and despair, between dying and rising, is acted out in the midst of Christ's people, as in Baptism and Eucharist we are made partakers of his death and resurrection. We immerse ourselves in the living water which gushes out from the rock; we are plunged into the mystery of new life which breaks out from the tomb.

In this book we have looked into the variety of ways in which this new life, drawn from death itself, has been lived and experienced, celebrated and sung through the centuries in Wales. 'I trust in your power, great is the deed you did once for all, you put down death, you put down hell, you put down Satan under your feet. May this never go from my mind.' This affirmation of Pantycelyn could not be more emphatic. To follow in this way, which Christ opens up to us through conflict and death, is, as Ann Griffiths declares, to follow in a way that not only justifies the sinner but also 'raises up the dead to life'. Already here and now, in the perplexities of this life, we taste the joy of the resurrection and find ourselves to be 'children of the resurrection'. All the barriers between earth and heaven, time and eternity, are being cast down.

That same assurance is heard in the poets of our own century, in Gwenallt and in Waldo Williams. But here there is a difference. There is both continuity and discontinuity with the heritage of the Methodist revival, for there are elements in that inheritance against which both writers react violently. Somehow in the nineteenth century the vision of Welsh Nonconformity seems to have hardened and narrowed. More and more the concentration on the cross as the centre of Christ's redeeming work seems to have obscured and even occluded the radiant affirmation of Easter. It seems that in Welsh Nonconformist thinking, the activity of God became increasingly limited to the sphere of 'religious experience' and 'religious institutions'. Liberating affirmations became imprisoning negations.

Of course, these tendencies were not characteristic of Welsh Nonconformity alone. They were characteristic, in various fashions, of many strands of Western Christianity, both Catholic and Protestant, in the nineteenth century. Gwenallt's and Waldo's reaction against them is remarkably deep. For both the resurrection is central; for neither is it possible to confine Christian faith to one specific area

The End which is a Beginning

of life. Waldo has his vision of the resurrection at work throughout the world of nature, present in each dawn. Gwenallt has his sense that the victory of life over death, which we see in Christ's rising from the tomb, is working itself out – sometimes consciously, sometimes not – in our contemporary struggles for justice and freedom in society.

This does not mean that, for Waldo, Easter is simply a reflection of the daily return of light, of the annual return of spring. Rather, it is these things which are pale reflections of that all-embracing, all-renewing power of life which is released in the mysterious breaking open of the tomb. Similarly, for Gwenallt, Christ's resurrection is not a mere reflection of our human efforts to attain justice and freedom. It is that eternal, disturbing power of divine love which is glimpsed in our human struggles for justice and truth, and in our ever-baffled longing to create something which is lasting and beautiful. This, for Gwenallt, is the flame which cannot be put out, because 'its light is the light of Easter morning, and upon its wick the fiery tongues of Pentecost are speaking'.

Thus in both Waldo and Gwenallt there is a kind of Christian humanism, a vision of human life as seen in the light of the resurrection. There is something which shines through their work. Herbert Hodges' words about Gwenallt could equally well apply to Waldo's writing:

> Gwenallt's religious poems ... breathe a kind of quiet joy; joy in mere existence, joy in God as the source of existence, joy in God's world, our place in it and the share which God himself has taken in our life here.

This joy, quiet but profound, is rooted in the conviction that the fabric of the world itself is shaped in a way which leads, in the end, through darkness into light, through conflict into harmony, through death into life. As an

Resurrection's Children

anonymous Irish writer expressed it back in the tenth century, the making of heaven and earth and the formation of the world

> was effected by Christ's resurrection from the dead on the eve of Easter. For every kind of matter, every element and every essence which is seen in the world were all combined in the body in which Christ arose, that is in the body of every human being.... All the world rose with him, for the essence of all the elements dwelt in the body which Jesus assumed.

This same conviction is matched in the work of the great medieval poets in their all-pervasive sense of the presence of the risen Lord throughout creation. Here we see a totally unselfconscious form of Christian humanism, an assurance that the gifts of grace do not destroy the gifts of nature but bring them to fulfilment and completion. This involves a new revelation of the latent ability of our ordinary, everyday human life to disclose some part of the glory and gentleness of the resurrection. Whether in the parish church at Oswestry, with its 'bright school of grace, its men of metre and grammar, handling God day by day' – or whether in the building of the house at Moelyrch, high on the hillside, looking down across the valley towards England – a place for God's habitation, a place for his indwelling, is being prepared. There is a divine potential which is revealed here; something which the unaided human heart and mind would never have suspected. A divine potential can be seen as the light of Easter touches our world at every point.

So, when Meilyr looks across the sound to Enlli and sees the island as a place which is in active expectation of the resurrection, he is telling us something not just about that particular place, however special it may be, but about all

The End which is a Beginning

places. All places are potentially holy, potentially open to the presence of the divine creative love, which overcomes death and reveals the resurrection. One of the great poets of the nineteenth century, who was also a Calvinistic Methodist minister, saw this potential as universal: *'mae'r oll yn gysegredig*; all, all is sacred.'[1] Everything is holy, capable of being consecrated to the God who, in his love, goes down to the deepest point of death and desolation, and in the deepest darkness reveals the divine power of his creative light. This light which shone at the beginning breaks down the barriers which sin and death have made. It opens the way forward into that communion of life, that participation in the eternal exchange of love which lies at the heart of God, Three-in-One.

Appendix

Things to Discuss and Places to Visit

Things to discuss

At the end of each chapter of this book there are some questions suggested for use by Lent groups. The topics provided are only suggestions and are not meant to restrict the development of the discussion. It may well be that in a small group where people know each other well, more personal topics will arise, and if so, this would be excellent.

It will be seen that Chapters 1 and 2 centre on questions about prayer, worship and the life of the Church; Chapters 3 and 4 look at our attitudes to our society and how we work with dissent and disagreement; and Chapters 5 and 6 bring us to questions about health and sickness and how we may learn to confront the journey towards death.

If there is a post-Easter meeting, it would be good if the group leader could get hold of the book *Lent, Holy Week and Easter*, which contains the revised services as set out for the use of the Church of England. This could be the basis for a discussion of the way in which the Holy Week services have been celebrated, and how it may be possible for more people to take part in them and to come to a deeper understanding of their meaning.

Things to Discuss and Places to Visit

Places to visit

This is a book which is full of places and people. I hope that it will make you want to get to know the people better and, if possible, to visit the places. Of course, how possible that will be depends to some extent on where you live. For example, people from South Wales are notoriously slow to visit North Wales, and vice versa. Visiting the holy places gives us a wonderful chance to cross these barriers.

If you live in England and have not yet done much exploring in Wales, you have a feast in front of you. Much, of course, depends on where you are coming from. For instance, it is much easier to visit a place in mid-Wales if you live in Birmingham, Manchester or Liverpool rather than Kent, Cornwall or Cumbria. But even so, distances in our island are not all that great, and there is no substitute for actually going to places and, if you can, walking at least the last bit of the way, and so giving yourself time to get the feel of the place.

Most of the churches mentioned in this Appendix will, I hope, be open, though some will be distinctly more welcoming than others! It goes without saying that the cathedral at St Davids is a church which is greatly visited; but the same is also true, at least in the summer, of much smaller places, such as the church at Aberdaron. One of the most striking places of pilgrimage at the present time is the church at Pennant Melangell, with its restored twelfth-century shrine – the oldest such shrine in Britain. But there are many other places which deserve your attention, places which will indeed come to new life precisely because you and other people visit them with prayer and expectation.

Resurrection's Children

Williams Pantycelyn

The church where Pantycelyn is buried is at Llanfair-ar-y-Bryn, about a mile from the centre of Llandovery (or Llanymddyfri), near the road which leads to Builth Wells (the A483). Pantycelyn's grave is in the churchyard to the north of the building. Pantycelyn, the farmhouse where he lived, is about five miles from Llanymddyfri and can be reached by turning off the Brecon road (the A40) at Ty-Gwyn.

A church connected with Pantycelyn is the old church of St Davids Llanwrtyd, which lies about a mile and a half north up the valley from the present town of Llanwrtyd Wells on the way to Abergwesyn. Here Pantycelyn served as a deacon in the very first years of his ministry. The church, which is always open, contains a fine wooden statue of St David, a fine engraving of Pantycelyn and a modern icon of the Holy Trinity, painted by the Revd Brian Bessant, the vicar of Llanwrtyd Wells. It is a memorial to a seventeen-year-old girl who was murdered in the valley a few years ago. It has helped to make the church a place of prayer for peace and reconciliation.

Ann Griffiths, Ruth Evans and Mary Jones

Llanfihangel-y-Pennant, the hamlet from which Mary Jones came, lies at the head of the valley running up from Tywyn in Meirionydd. The church where she was baptized and the ruins of the cottage where she was brought up are still to be seen. Her grave is in the churchyard of the Calvinistic Methodist chapel in Bryn-crug, three miles down the valley. This is an exceptionally beautiful part of Wales, and the churches at Tywyn and Llanegryn are well

Things to Discuss and Places to Visit

worth visiting. The patron saint of Tywyn is St Cadfan, one of the founding fathers of Enlli (Bardsey Island).

Ann Griffiths lies buried in the churchyard at Llanfihangel-yng-Gwynfa, just off the road from Llanfyllin to Lake Efyrnwy (the B4393), the church where she was baptized and married. There is an Ann Griffiths memorial chapel three miles to the south at Dolanog, with striking sculptured heads of Ann and John Hughes in it. John's chapel at Pontrobert, where the Methodists met in Ann's lifetime, has been recently restored as an ecumenical centre for Christian prayer and renewal. John and his wife Ruth are buried nearby. For more information about the centre contact Nia Rhosier (tel: 01938 500631). For information about Llanfihangel-yng-Gwynfa contact the vicar, the Revd Sidney Gilbert (tel: 01691 870663).

In Bala there is a statue of Thomas Charles outside the Presbyterian chapel. Charles and his wife lie buried in the churchyard at Llanycil on the edge of Lake Bala, two miles to the west.

Gwenallt and Waldo

There is a memorial to Gwenallt and two of his contemporaries in the centre of Pontardawe, where he was born and grew up. There is a memorial stone to Waldo outside the village of Mynachlog-Ddu in the Preseli Hills. But to remember Waldo it is perhaps best to go to St Davids and to the country immediately around the city. St Davids is the smallest cathedral city in Britain and the holiest shrine in Wales.

To remember the poet Gwenallt, who longed to bring people of all kinds into God's Church, you cannot do better than to visit Penrhys in the Rhondda. This is the site of an ancient shrine to Our Lady, now restored. It is also the site of a remarkable and inventive ecumenical venture in Christian community living, directed by the Revd John Morgans, a former moderator of the United Reformed Church. It serves one of the most deprived council estates in South Wales and is without question one of the truly hopeful signs of our time. For further information: tel: 01443 756754.

Guto'r Glyn and Meilyr Brydydd

We do not know where Guto was born, but the house of his friend and patron, or at least the present successor of the house, can still be seen on the hillside in the valley of Llansilin. The shrine of St Melangell, to which Hywel was exhorted to go, is about twelve miles away. It is two miles up the valley from Llangynog, where you turn off the road from Llanfyllin to Bala (B4391). Visit the church, with its remarkable restored shrine, and also visit the nearby Cancer Help Centre. For further information: tel: 01691 860408.

Meilyr Brydydd prayed to go to Ynys Enlli (Bardsey Island). The crossing to the island is still not easy. Regular crossings are made on Saturdays, but only for those who have booked accommodation for the week on the island. In the summer it is often possible to get a boat which will make the crossing for the day. But even without going to the island, you can see it clearly from the end of the Llŷn Peninsula, beyond Aberdaron. You can also visit the parish church at Aberdaron, where the poet R. S. Thomas was for some years the vicar. It is a remarkable building, situated almost on the beach. This was the land-base for the island community on Bardsey in the days before the Reformation. For further information about staying on the island contact Simon Glyn (tel: 01758 730740).

Notes

Chapter 1: Cheerfully Towards Jerusalem

1. *English Hymnal*, No. 397.
2. In Welsh the hymn can be found in *Emynau'r Eglwys* (Cardiff, 1959), No. 340.
3. Eifion Evans, *Pursued by God* (Bridgend, 1996), p. 31.
4. Gomer M. Roberts, *Y Per Ganiedydd* (Llandysul, 1949), Vol. 1, pp. 82-3.
5. Evans, op. cit., p. 30.
6. *Llyfr Emynau a Thonau* (Caernarfon, 1929), No. 681.
7. R. M. Jones, *Cyfrinaeth Gymraeg* (Llandysul, 1995), pp. 78-132, particularly pp. 113-17.
8. *Llyfr Emynau a Thonau*, op. cit., No. 589, v. 2.
9. Ibid., No. 678. On this infinite growth into the life of God, a great medieval Greek theologian, St Gregory Palamas, writes: 'But we do not know and have never heard of anyone from the beginning of time who having received this vision while on earth does not desire still more perfect vision. Thus, since the desire of those who have received this vision is limitless, since the grace already granted them gives them power to receive greater vision, since He who gives himself is infinite and bestows himself abundantly and lavishly, how can the sons of the age to come not progress infinitely in this vision, acquiring grace after grace and joyfully ascending the ascent which never wearies?' G. I. Mantzaridis, *The Deification of Man:*

St Gregory Palamas and The Orthodox Tradition (New York, 1984), p. 125.
10. It is easy to see why Tolkien had such a love for the Welsh language, and used elements from it in making the languages for *The Lord of the Rings*.

Chapter 2: Companions on the Way

1. Gwyn Alf Williams, *Madoc: The Making of a Myth* (London, 1979), p. 94.
2. In all that relates to Mary Jones I am deeply indebted to my friend E. Wyn James.
3. See E. Wyn James, 'Ann Griffith, Mary Jones a Mecca'r Methodistiaid.' *Llên Cymru* 21, (1998).
4. For the life of Ann Griffiths see A. M. Allchin, *Ann Griffiths, the Furnace and the Fountain* (Cardiff, 1987).
5. R. D. Williams, *After Silent Centuries* (Oxford, 1994), p. 44.
6. Alan Gaunt, *Always From Joy, Hymn Texts 1991–1996* (London, 1997).
7. John Morgan of Mold. I have drawn much on the two articles which he published at the turn of the last century, one in *Y Drysorfa 1898*, pp. 355–60, and the other in *Cymru 1905*, pp. 29–36.
8. Gaunt, op. cit., p. 85.
9. Ibid., p. 84.
10. H. A. Hodges, *Homage to Ann Griffiths: A Special Bicentenary Publication* (Cardiff, 1976), p. 13.

Chapter 3: The Harvest of Maturity

1. For the life and work of Waldo Williams see the study by James Nicholas in the 'Writers of Wales' series (Cardiff, 1975).
2. In this chapter I am making use of Tony Conran's mas-

Notes

terly book of translations from Waldo Williams, *The Peacemakers* (Gomer Press, Llandysul, 1997). This book, with its introduction as well as its translations, makes Waldo accessible in English in a quite new way.
3. A. M. Allchin, *Praise Above All: Discovering the Welsh Tradition* (Cardiff, 1991), pp. 142ff.
4. J. Nicholas (ed.), *Waldo: Teyrnged* (Llandysul, 1977), p. 11.
5. From a translation of 'Tŷ Ddewi' made by Professor Dafydd Johnston and included in Conran's book, op. cit. p. 191.
6. Henry Vaughan, *The Complete Poems*, ed. Alan Rudrum (London, 1978), p. 193.
7. Conran, op. cit., p. 205.
8. Ibid., p. 145.
9. See James Nicholas, *Waldo Williams* (Cardiff, 1975), p. 81.
10. Conran, op. cit., pp. 169–71.
11. See the article by David Ford in *Encounter with Mystery: Reflections on L'Arche and Living with Disability*, ed. Frances Young (London, 1997), p. 82.
12. Conran, op. cit., p. 43.
13. Ibid., p. 46.
14. A. M. Allchin, op. cit., p. 35.

Chapter 4: On the Roads of Wales

1. For an English introduction to Gwenallt see Dyfnallt Morgan's book on Gwenallt in the 'Writers of Wales' series (Cardiff, 1972).
2. In this chapter I make use of H. A. Hodges' unpublished translations of Gwenallt's poems and also of his notes on the writer which are in my possession.
3. Donald Nicholl, *The Testing of Hearts* (London, Revised edition, 1998) pp. 9–13.

4. From the article on Gwenallt in *The Oxford Companion to the Literature of Wales* (Oxford, 1986), p. 299.
 5. Original in *Gwreiddiau* (Llandysul, 1959), pp. 22–3.
 6. Original in *Ysgubau'r Awen* (Llandysul, 1938), p. 85.
 7. Original in J. E. Meredith, *Gwenallt, Bardd Crefyddol* (Llandysul, 1974), p. 78. An English translation of this essay was published in *Planet*, No. 32, 1976.
 8. Original in *Eples* (Llandysul, 1951), pp. 63–4.
 9. Original in *Gwreiddiau*, op. cit., p. 55.
10. Seamus Heaney, *The Government of the Tongue: The 1986 T. S. Eliot Memorial Lectures and Other Critical Writings* (London, 1988), p. 38.
11. *Gwreiddiau*, op. cit., p. 52.
12. There is a valuable discussion of these questions in the chapter on Gwenallt in Bobi Jones' book *Crist a Chenedlaetholdeb* (Bridgend, 1994). The writer looks at Gwenallt's fusion of evangelicalism and sacramentalism and sees it as a sign of true ecumenism, and places it in relation to his understanding of the Christian significance of national identity. There is material here which I hope to follow up in more detail in a forthcoming publication.
13. Original in *Y Coed* (Llandysul, 1969), p. 26.

Chapter 5: Stages of Life's Journey

 1. A brief account of Pennant Melangell can be found in *Pennant Melangell – Place of Pilgrimage*, available from the shrine shop, Pennant Melangell, Llangynog via Oswestry.
 2. A. O. H. Jarman and Gwilym Rees Hughes (eds), *A Guide to Welsh Literature, Vol. II* (Swansea, 1979), p. 219.
 3. Richard Loomis and Dafydd Johnston, *Medieval Welsh Poems: An Anthology Translation and Commentary* (Binghampton, NY, 1992), pp. 175–6. This anthology

Notes

contains translations of twenty-six of Guto'r Glyn's poems. I am deeply grateful to Richard Loomis for all his help and encouragement, and particularly for allowing me to make use of his translations of, and work on the poetry of Guto, as yet unpublished.

4. Ibid., pp. 157–9. See also on this poem R. M. Jones, *Llên Cymru a Chrefydd* (Abertawe, 1977), pp. 289–90.
5. Ibid., pp. 159–61.
6. Andrew Breeze, *Medieval Welsh Literature* (Dublin, 1997), p. 27. But see the writer's comment on this whole question, pp. 25–7.
7. Again I am relying on an unpublished translation by Richard Loomis.

Chapter 6: The Isle of Expectation

1. A. M. Allchin, *Bardsey, A Place of Pilgrimage* (Aberdaron, 1991), pp. 4–5.
2. Gerald of Wales, *The Journey Through Wales*, translated by Lewis Thorpe (London, 1978), pp. 183–4.
3. The poems of Meilyr and his family are to be found in the following volume of the series 'The Poets of the Princes', produced by the Centre for Higher Celtic Studies in the University of Wales in Aberystwyth: J. E. Caerwyn Williams and Peredur I. Lynch (eds), *Gwaith Meilyr Brydydd a'i Ddisgynyddion* (Cardiff, 1994).
4. From the article by J. E. Caerwyn Williams, 'Meilyr Brydydd and Gruffudd ap Cynan' in *Gruffud ap Cynan: A Collaborative Biography*, ed. K. L. Maund (Woodbridge, 1996), p. 176.
5. Ibid., pp. 174–5. It is striking to find this same word *cerennydd* occurring in the final line of a poem written by Meilyr's grandson, Meilyr ap Gwalchmai, 'May I have the friendship of the Lord forever'. For the poem and a commentary on it see Oliver Davies, *Celtic Christianity in*

Resurrection's Children

Early Medieval Wales: The Origins of the Welsh Spiritual Tradition (Cardiff, 1996), pp. 103–5.
6. Quoted in Paul Bryant-Quinn's article on the interpretation of the *marwysgafn*. See *Llên Cymru*, cyfrol 20, 1997, pp. 12–24. I have gained much in my understanding of this poem in conversation with the writer, whose insights are always illuminating.
7. Ibid.
8. Translation by Joseph Clancy in *The Oxford Book of Welsh Verse in English* (Oxford, 1977), pp. 20–21.
9. See p. 6 above.
10. K. L. Maund, op. cit., p. 76.
11. Gerard Casey, *Night Horizons* (Dorchester, 1997), p. 226.